A SLOW SCREW AGAINST THE WALL

... AND OTHER COCKTAILS

TAKE THAT BOOKS

Take That Books is an imprint of
Take That Ltd.
P.O.Box 200
Harrogate
HG1 4XB

Copyright © 1994 Take That Books

Written by Sam Weren
Illustrated by Clyde

Australian Associate:
MaxiBooks, P.O.Box 529, Kiama, NSW 2533, Australia.

10 9 8 7 6 5 4 3 2 1

ISBN 1-873668-60-0

Layout and typesetting by
Impact Design, P.O.Box 200, Harrogate, HG1 4XB.

Printed and bound in Great Britain.

Open to Temptation?

The cocktail has acquired a definite suggestive quality over the years. Where a beer is synonymous with going out on the town and wine is associated with a delicious meal, the cocktail somehow oozes sexual overtones.

Cocktails have most traditionally been served as aperitifs to stimulate gastric juices. However, the last ten years have seen a movement towards serving cocktails as digestifs to stimulate a totally different set of juices.

Naturally this has been shown in the names applied to the recipes of the more famous cocktail chefs. Where Stingers, Manhattans and Flips pervaded, we can now witness a movement towards *Kisses in the Dark, Slow Screws* and *Groin Bangers*.

Whether these suggestive names do any more than 'suggest', only you can know. The soporific and flaccidity inducing qualities of alcohol are well documented, so too much of a good thing can definitely be a bad thing.

It is possible to buy ready mixed cocktails from off-licences, or to persuade your local pub to serve a cocktail instead of a pint of 'best'. Whilst these could be nice, there is nothing quite like doing it for yourself.

Within the pages of *A Slow Screw Against the Wall and Other Cocktails* you'll find many helpful hints and tips from old-campaigners. These are all designed to improve your cocktail parties, if not your sex life. Before long you'll assume the air of an 'old hand'.

The sensual skills of many cocktail pioneers have been documented to provide a blue print for sheer enjoyment. You'll find everything you need including which glasses to use, how to prepare your fruit and how to mix

"Who's for a Groin Banger, then?"

the drinks. On top of that, there is a list of useful equipment for preparing your drinks, descriptions of over 50 different liqueurs, and details of how to prepare your garnishes.

But by far the largest part of the book is dedicated to succulent cocktail recipes. Old favourites rub shoulders with tasty upstarts. Long, cool, lazy highballs sit next to powerful shorts. And mysterious clear concoctions vie with colourful works of art. Whatever your tastes, with over 250 to choose from, you'll find something to set your senses on fire. Bonne soirée!

What do you want?

COCKTAIL (Cok'tail), n. drink of spirit with bitters, sugar, etc. (origin doubtful; from U.S.).

SLOW (-), a., adv., & v. Not quick, deficient of speed, taking a long time to do a thing.

SCREW (-oo), n., & v.t. & i. Oblique curling motion or tendency.

WALL (wawl), n., Continuous and usually vertical and solid structure of stones, bricks, concrete, timber, etc., narrow in proportion to length & height. Serving to enclose, protect or divide.

THE RIGHT EQUIPMENT

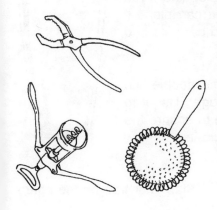

When it comes to giving pleasure to others by mixing your own cocktails, there's nothing to beat using your own equipment. Of course, it is always possible to borrow the right tools from a friend, or even hire a set from your off-licence, but neither will give you as much joy getting your own utensils dirty.

You'll need the following equipment for your bar:

Double-ended measuring cup: Also called a double-jigger, a pourer or a tot. This is necessary to measure the exact amount of liquid for your drinks. The most useful size is 15ml and 30ml, to measure ½ part and 1 part respectively.

Fruit-squeezer: This is a useful tool for extracting fresh juice from fruit. It can save you a lot of time over hand squeezing.

Mixing spoon: These have a long handle for use in all shapes of glasses including highballs. Make sure you buy one with a rough or twisted handle. Smooth handles can become very slippery when they get wet.

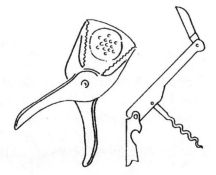

Professional bar shaker with a wire strainer: There are two main types of cocktail shaker; the standard three-piece and the Boston two-piece. The former has a strainer built into the top section,

whilst the Boston breaks near the middle. Avoid damaging the lid and wrap the shaker in a towel when at work. You wouldn't want your drink to spurt over your guests prematurely.

Strainer: If your shaker doesn't have a strainer, you may find a hawthorn strainer useful. You can place it over the front of your strainer or jug to hold back ice and other unwanted solids such as fruit pips.

570ml glass jug with pouring lip: Some people like bigger jugs, but this size is plenty big enough. Use it to stir your cocktails, and keep it in the fridge to ensure the contents are kept cool. The lips should be narrow enough to hold back the ice.

Cutting board: To prepare fruit for drinks. Slap your fruit on the board and chop away.

Sharp fruit knife: Keep it small, you don't want a big chopper.

Insulated ice bucket, ice crusher and ice tongs: For storing your ice in case you get too hot. If you can't find a crusher, place your ice cubes in a tea-towel and smack your bits with a hammer. Be careful where you drop those cubes.

Corkscrew: Old fashioned hand screws are the best. Modern ones may incorporate a bottle opener which is useful for opening beer and mixer bottles.

Zester: For extracting the zest from fruit peel.

Electric blender: One of the most useful items in your armoury. Choose one with multi-speeds and capable of blending ice cubes. Keep it clean or it will begin to smell.

Bowls: A couple of bowls will be needed for keeping your fruits and garnishes.

Seals: For wine, champagne and mixer bottles when you want to keep the contents fresh.

Tassles: Or additional bits and pieces. You'll need serviettes, coasters, toothpicks, straws, swizzle sticks and cloths.

Finally, you'll need some open-minded fun-loving guests all eager to taste your latest concoctions and anything else you may have to offer!

WHO WAS FIRST?

Some experts say the first recipe for a cocktail was a concoction of lemon juice and powdered adders called Vinigallici. It was prepared by the physician Claudius in the second century AD. Although intended to be a medicine, the drink was highly praised by Emperor Commodus as an aperitif!

Certainly the ancient Greeks mixed their wine with resin to produce a drink with a more interesting flavour called Retsina. It also had the effect of preserving the wine.

The modern cocktail started life in America during the prohibition when all forms of liquor were illegal. What alcohol was available from the underworld, called 'hooch', had a pretty foul taste

"Friends, countrymen, Dirty Mothers..."

and needed improving before it could be stomached. Many creative brains were put to use inventing suitable mixtures and these drinks became known as cocktails.

It is generally accepted that the American cocktail crossed the Atlantic in the 1930s and became popular at society dinners in Europe.

A man returned early from work to find his wife scrubbing the kitchen floor. The rhythmic movement of her body over the tiles gave him uncontrollable sensual ideas. Dropping his trousers, he lifted his wife's skirt and mounted straight away. Five minutes later they both collapsed in a heap of satisfaction. The man pulled up his trousers and the wife returned to her scrubbing. Suddenly the man turned round and kicked his wife gently on the bum. "Ouch," she protested, "how can you do that when we've just had so much pleasure together?" "That," he retorted, "is for not turning round to see who it was!"

DIRTY JIGGERS AND BIG PARTS

To avoid passing on infection, you should always keep your jigger as clean as possible! And that goes for all your measuring implements, however big they are. Don't let people tell you that size isn't important. When it comes to cocktails, the exact volume is of upmost importance. But how much is one 'part'? And how can you measure a 'dash'?

A dash = ¼ teaspoon = approx 10 drops

1 part = 1 jigger = 30ml = 1oz = 1 pony

A wine glass (in this book) = 25ml = 4oz

A Miniature = 1 parts = 1.6oz = 50ml

A pinch = 1/6th teaspoon = 1/36th ounce

You should be able to squeeze 26 parts out of a spirit bottle and six to eight servings from a bottle of wine.

If you are holding a party, allow for three drinks per person, equivalent to around a half bottle of wine.

THE ART OF MIXING COCKTAILS

 Making love and making cocktails are very similar; they take a lifetime to master, but even a novice can muddle their way through. Follow a few simple rules and you'll have your guests groaning with pleasure. And they might like your cocktails as well!...

Before starting to mix your drinks, make sure all your bits are in one place - near you. You'll want to have prepared as much as possible before the show begins.

Special glasses are not really necessary. Almost any container, from a coconut shell to an old bucket, can be used to hold a cocktail attractively. As a guideline, however, choose stemmed glasses for cocktails which are not served on ice, as they will stay cooler for longer. Tumblers or highball glasses are better for drinks which require ice. Short cocktails look their best in traditional triangular cocktail glasses. While goblet styles are generally used for drinks incorporating egg yolks.

Make sure all your glasses are clean. There's nothing like picking up a Between the Sheets for appreciation and finding sticky stains distorting your view - what a turn off.

All cocktails are best served cold. It makes a great difference if the glasses have been chilled. Ideally the glasses should stand in the refrigerator for an hour or two before needed, but a scoop of ice placed in the glass and left there while the drink is being prepared will chill it very effectively.

Follow the recipes as closely as possible and use the best ingredients available. Juices should be at least half PURE fruit juice, or they will simply water your cocktail down. Even a slight variation in quantities of fruit or alcohol can drastically alter the flavour of the drink.

Prepare lots of ice before the party. Have it ready for use, cut into cubes or crushed in a bowl.

When everything's ready for action, and your guests are gagging for it, step into the limelight and do your bit...

SHAKE IT, SQUEEZE IT, STIR IT AND STRAIN IT.

Shaking

This method is usual for sweet-and-sour, sweet and cream-type drinks.

Place the ice into the shaker first, allowing the ingredients to be cooled as they are added. You can use either crushed or cubed ice. Always add the alcohol ingredients last.

Never fill your shaker to the brim. You should leave some room for everything to mix easily. Approximately three-quarters full is a good guideline.

Shake briskly by hand and serve as soon as the outside of the shaker begins to sweat. A few recipes ask for longer shakes, but don't overdo it or you'll be too tired to carry on. In general, the longer the shake, the colder the drink.

Squeezing

Of course, you don't squeeze your cocktails, but you should squeeze your own fruit for mixers. Processed juices just don't have the same effect.

Whenever you can, choose fresh, plump, ripe fruit for your cocktails. Always squeeze them gently, taking care not to spurt your juice everywhere. Use the palm of your hand and contract your fingers rhythmically, until your fruit is spent.

Stirring

This is for Martini-type drinks where you want to make sure the base spirit is not bruised. Pour the ingredients into a 570ml glass jug with a pouring lip, then stir with a clean bar spoon. Use ice blocks, not chips, and serve immediately before the ice dilutes the mixture. If the lip of the jug does not hold the ice cubes back, you may have to use a Hawthorn strainer.

In the Northern hemisphere, you should stir in an anti-clockwise direction. In the Southern hemisphere, stir in the opposite, clockwise direction.

Floating

This is done when a recipe calls for a cream or high-proof spirit to be floated on top of the mixed ingredients. Take a warm bar spoon (or a curved dessert spoon), hold it upside-down so the bottom touches the side of the glass just above the other ingredients, then carefully pour the spirit or cream over it.

Straining

Most people choose to strain their home-made cocktails through the kitchen sieve normally reserved for peas or corn. However, it is better to invest in a proper cocktail strainer which will fit over the mouth of your shaker. This should ensure no unwanted detritus such as cherry stalks, orange pips or even peas get into your lovingly prepared drink.

It is not advised to 'add flavour' by using your three day old socks or stockings, no matter how many cocktails you've already downed.

Blending

If your recipe calls for a mixture of fresh fruit or eggs, they will need to be blended to give them a frothy consistency. Pour the ingredients together with ice into an electric blender, then blend briefly.

Muddling

Use the back or edge of your stirring spoon to squash pieces of fruit, leaves and/or sugar cubes against the edge of the glass. This will squeeze the flavour out of them and help blend the cocktail.

Frosting

Frosting a glass is totally different to chilling a glass! To frost a glass, hold it upside down and rub a slice of lemon or lime around the rim. Then take the glass, still upside down, and dip it into a bowl of salt or sugar. Twist the glass to ensure a good coating, and remove.

Once you have become proficient at frosting you can experiment with various colours. Instead of rubbing the lemon around the rim, dip the glass into a shallow saucer of Creme de Cassis, Grenadine or similar coloured liqueur. Other 'frosts' include beaten egg-white, coconut, coffee and cocoa powder.

Building

With this method, you 'build' your cocktail in the glass as opposed to in a jug or shaker. Add the densest ingredient first and float each subsequent ingredient on top of it. You will have to pour slowly, so the various ingredients don't mix in the glass. A cocktail built by an expert can look amazing as well as tasting fantastic. As you work your way down the drink, you experience each flavour on its own and then mixed slightly with adjacent layers.

And a few more tips...

- Never put carbonated ingredients into your shaker, mixing glass or liquidiser.

- Glasses should not be filled to the brim and remember to leave room for your garnish.

- Cocktails should be served fresh as they will separate if left too long.

- Always hold the glass by the stem or the base to avoid fingerprints and unnecessary warming of the drink.

- Use top quality ingredients.

- Transfer canned ingredients to clean bottles and seal them to keep the contents fresh.

DID YOU KNOW... An official from the New York Bartenders Union claims that even the best bartenders can only remember around 50 different cocktails.

Stock The Basics

If you are new to mixing cocktails, the startling array of ingredients can leave you wondering how many millions of pounds you are going to have to spend. Fear not. The majority of cocktails can be made with a relatively few number of ingredients. A recommended core stock would include:

Whisky
Gin
Vodka
Brandy
Angostura bitters
Soda water
Lemonade
Ginger beer
Tomato juice
Crème de Cassis
Curacao (blue)
Grenadine
Crème de Menthe (green)
Vermouth
Sugar syrup

For garnishes you'll need lemons, limes, oranges, eggs and cherries.

A company boss was expecting to go home for a quiet birthday with his family. Then, just before it was time to leave, his desirable secretary asked him if he wanted to come back to her flat for a drink. Having fantasised for years about his secretary, he couldn't accept quick enough.

Back at the flat, they had a couple of drinks and then the secretary said she needed to go into her bedroom to 'see to a few things'. On her way she dimmed the lights and looked back with a smile on her face. The boss could stand it no longer. He took off all his clothes and rushed towards the bedroom door. Just before he got there, the door burst open. "Happy birthday to you," sang his wife, children, work mates and several friends.

THE TALE BEHIND THE COCKTAIL

So where does the word 'cocktail' come from? There are many stories, some more plausible than others. Here is the pick of the best...

❏ The first involves an Aztec overlord in Mexico whose beautiful daughter was called Xoctl. Some American naval officers went to visit her father and, after a pleasant meeting, were served some exotic mixed drinks. The officers said they would never forget Xoctl, so they decided to name the drinks after her. The closest they could come to pronouncing her name was "Cock~tail" and a legend was born.

❏ Another story comes from the American War of Independence. An innkeeper named Betsy Flanagan, whose premises were frequented by Washington's officers and their French allies, once prepared a meal of chickens she stole from a pro-British neighbour. To celebrate this small victory she decorated glasses used at the feast with feathers plucked from the chickens. Her French clients heartily toasted her with cries of "Vive le cock-tail"!

❏ Still in the War of Independence, another story revolves around the daughter of a patriotic innkeeper. The man's desire was to see his beloved Bessie marry an American soldier called Jake. Determined to show her own independence, Bessie refused. At around the same time, the innkeepers prize fighting cock, patriotically called 'Washington' went missing. So, he came up with the idea that the person to find and return Washington would receive his daughter's hand in marriage.

Not surprisingly it was Jake who found Washington. So delighted was the innkeeper that he had got his own way that he threw a feast to celebrate the betrothal. At the banquet Bessie was asked to serve the drinks. Realising she had been conned, she mixed the drinks in such way so as to cause an upset. But yet again her plans went awry. The revellers found them most satisfactory and Jake named them 'cock tails' in the memory of Washington.

❑ In 18th century England fighting cocks were given potent spirits to help them put up a 'good show' (cock ale). Any left overs were used by the victors in their celebrations, to which the tails of the losing cocks were added.

❑ A New Orleans pharmacist called William Pechaud allowed the local Freemasons to use his home for their meetings. After the serious business he would give them all a mixture of brandy, bitters and sugar. These were all served in double-ended gallic egg-cups called coquetiers.

❑ British sailors visiting Campeche in the Gulf of Mexico were served a delicious punch by the local bar owners. One of the ingredients was a distinctively shaped root called Cola de Gallo. The closest translation they could manage was 'cocktail'.

❑ (Linking the recurrent French and American War of Independence themes) The Marquis de Lafayette recruited several hundred mercenaries to travel with him and to fight the British in America. These volunteers, mostly from the Bordeaux region, brought wine cups with them which were known as coquetel.

❑ Gamblers on the Mississippi steamboats were given the run of the bar when they had a particularly successful evening. A tub shaped like a cock's breast would be produced and samples from every liquor bottle behind the bar would be poured in. The stirring implement used to mix the drinks was shaped like a cock's tail, hence...

❑ Perhaps one of the more likely involves the tails of horses. Non-thoroughbreds, those of mixed stock, would have their tales docked. These were known as 'cock-tailed' horses. Therefore any mixed drink, not pure spirit, also became known as a cock-tail.

WHICH WAY DO YOU SWING?

Cocktails have a language all their own and many drinks can be categorised. Which of these sets your imagination on fire?:

Cocktail: A basic liquor probably served with vermouth, bitters and fruit flavours. Always served cold.

Collins: Gin, rum, whisky or brandy with lemon or lime juice and soda water.

Cooler: A summer drink. Long, iced, cool drink made from sherry or wine, lemon and sugar plus soda water.

Flip: A drink made with eggs plus whisky, brandy or rum.

Frappe: A drink served with cracked ice.

Highball: Any spirit served with ice, soda water, lemonade, ginger beer or cola.

Julep: Bourbon whisky with fresh mint.

Mull: Punch made with hot wine.

On the rocks: Any drink served with cubed ice.

Punch: Wines, spirits and fruit juices mixed with spices and sugar. Often served warm.

Sling: Gin, rum or whisky with dissolved sugar, lemon or lime juice and bitters poured over ice.

Sour: Spirits shaken with lemon or lime juice and usually the white of an egg.

Straight up: A drink served without ice.

Strain: Pour mix through strainer to remove ice particles and fruit.

Toddy: A spirit, hot water and cinnamon, cloves, nutmeg and/or lemon peel.

Twist: A drink containing a small strip of lemon peel. The strip is sharply twisted to bruise the rind; this allows oil to escape into the drink when the peel is floated.

REMEMBER: All cocktails must be measured carefully and as long as the measure remains constant throughout the recipe, the drink will have the correct flavour and consistency.

TOP COCKTAILS

More cocktails are drunk in the USA than any other country. So the top 10 is naturally tilted towards American preferences.

1.	Dry Martini	6.	Old Fashioned
2.	Gin & Tonic	7.	Bloody Mary
3.	John Collins	8.	Pina Colada
4.	Screwdriver	9.	Singapore Sling
5.	Manhattan	10.	Tequila Sunrise

HOOKERS AND SLAMMERS

Two drinks favoured by those short on time are the Tequila Slammer and the Tequila Hooker. Both are designed to get the alcohol into your system as rapidly as possible. The Slammer uses the well-known technique of mixing strong alcohol with bubbles. Whilst the Hooker opens the pores on your tongue with salt, pours in the tequila and closes the pores with lemon.

Great care must be taken with both of these concoctions. It will only take a few MINUTES for the tequila to reach your nervous system. However, it only takes but a few SECONDS to drink either, since the art depends on speed. So, you should not be tempted to Slam or Hook a few down until you know what's happening to your system.

Both of these drinks are firm favourites with the ski-bums who hang around the Alps during the winter months. Here, the altitude and the rarer oxygen levels have their own effects.

This is how they go:-

THE SLAMMER

Wham

Wham approximately two-thirds of lemonade into a thick bottomed beaker.

Bam

Bam in two large measures of tequila.

Thank you Mam

Cover the top of the beaker with your hand. Raise the beaker approximately five

centimetres above the table and slam it down hard. As the mixture starts to fizz, drink it down in one. Now, cross your eyes, lie back and think of Mexico.

THE HOOKER

The following stages should be taken in quick succession. Take care not to suck when you should be licking, or to swallow too early - these are punishable offences in some parts of the world!

Lick

Take a pinch of salt and place it on the back of your hand, then lick it with the tip of your tongue.

Swallow

Take a double shot of tequila and drink it in one go.

Suck

Grab a fresh slice of lemon and bite into it, quickly sucking the bitter juice.

A n old man was passing a playground one day when he spotted a sad looking youngster sat on the grass by himself crying his eyes out. Stooping down with a smile on his face, the old man asked the youngster what was wrong. The little boy looked up into the friendly face and complained "I'm sad because I can't do what the big boys do." The old man promptly sat down next to the youngster and started crying his eyes out.

GARNISHES

 A garnish should enhance a drink without disguising it. It can be anything from a floating flower to a stuffed green olive speared on a cocktail stick.

Slices of lemon, orange and lime are the most frequently used garnishes, along with cocktail cherries. Spear the garnish on a coloured swizzle stick. With tropical fruit drinks, garnish with fruits such as pineapple, mango and kiwifruit.

Savory garnishes include pearl onions, cucumber slices and stuffed olives together with sprigs of fresh mint. Celery salt and paprika are sometimes sprinkled over the finished drink before serving.

An attractive way to enhance a sweet cocktail is to frost the glass by dipping the rim of the glass in lemon and then sugar. Sour drinks may be frosted by dipping in salt crystals (see 'frosting' on page 13).

Creamy cocktails in particular can be garnished with a topping. Try sprinkling grated chocolate, ground coffee beans (powdered instant coffee is a reasonable alternative), grated nutmeg or ground cinnamon onto your drink. Little curls of chocolate is an alternative to the more usual 'cappuccino' look. Take a potato peeler and drag it along a bar of solid chocolate to produce short curls.

Of course, fruit is the most usual garnish in the cocktail sphere. Here's how to prepare your fruit so as to enhance and not hide your latest alcoholic creation.

Oranges/Lemons/Limes

These citrus fruits make ideal garnishes for most drinks. But because of their familiarity, you may like to try a couple of simple tricks instead of slapping a wedge into the glass.

Slices

The most simple, and often overlooked, is a plain slice. Take your fruit and drag a potato peeler across the skin, from top to bottom, to expose the pith without releasing any juice. Leave around 5mm of skin between the scores.

Next, lay the fruit on its side and cut across the fruit with a sharp knife starting at the middle. Then cut a slice approximately 2 or 3mm in width. The finished slice will have a serrated look, a bit like a cog.

Take a cocktail stick and push it through one side of the slice near to the edge. Then curl the slice slightly and push the stick through the opposite edge. You can now balance the stick across the rim of your drink. As a variation, try putting a cherry on the stick between the edges of the fruit slice. If you are short of fruit, use half slices in a similar manner.

Spirals

Using a potato peeler, cut into the skin of your fruit, not quite deep enough to touch the pith. Drag the peeler across the skin to produce a strip of peel approximately 3mm wide. As you go round the fruit, you'll find the strip will start to twist into a spiral. Continue until you have around 10 to 15cm of skin.

To garnish your drink, drop one end of the spiral into the drink and place the other end over the rim of the glass.

Knots

As above, use your peeler to remove a thin strip of peel from the fruit. This time make the strip a little wider, around 5mm. Cut a strip 10cm in length. Make several strips from one fruit.

Put down your peeler and select one of the strips. Now, gently tie it in a knot. Start with the most simple of single knots, and progress as you get the hang of it. You'll need a lot of practice and a longer strip of skin to form any sailor's knot.

Simply drop your knots into your drink. Alternatively use in conjunction with a slice of a different fruit on a cocktail stick.

Pineapple

Take a slice of pineapple through the middle of the fruit. Then cut it into quarters or eights. With your knife, cut into the bottom of the section, and push the fruit onto the rim of the glass.

Treat the leaves in a similar manner - slicing them at the bottom and inserting over the rim of your glass. Alternatively, pierce a couple of small leaves with a cocktail stick near the bottom and spear them into a strawberry or slice of pineapple.

Melons

You can buy special melon scoops. These look like miniature versions of ice-cream scoops. The balls can be skewered with a cocktail stick and hung across a glass.

If you have one, buy two or three different coloured melons and alternate the colours of the balls on the stick for more effect.

Bananas

You'll need firm bananas which have only just ripened. Without peeling the fruit, cut slices around 3mm thick. When you've made a few slices, take a handful and drop them into a cup containing lime or lemon juice. Apart from adding an interesting flavour, this will prevent the banana from becoming sullied.

Cut the slices so you can put them on the rim of a glass or add to a cocktail stick with a cherry or piece of strawberry.

Strawberries

The simplest garnish made with a strawberry is made by cutting the fruit in two from top to bottom leaving the leaves on top.

If you want something a bit fancier you could make a strawberry fan. As above, cut your strawberry in half. Next, cut the half from the bottom up to the top of the red fruit, but take care not to cut the leaves. Repeat this exercise four or five times. When finished, gently fan out the thin slices of strawberry using the leaves as a pivot.

Coconuts

Drill two small holes into your coconut and drain out the milk. Keep this for use in a cocktail or as a pleasant drink on its own. Then use anything you've got, and a great deal of strength or cunning, to break open your coconut.

Once opened, scrape off thin pieces of the flesh with a sharp knife. These will curl up as they dry and they can be dropped into your drink or balanced on the rim of your glass.

One coconut will usually do for more than one drinks party. So, try grating the remaining pieces and storing in a jar, or sprinkle them on top of a creamy drink.

ON THE ROCKS

Nobody can describe cocktail drinkers as impotent or frigid. Quite the opposite, they normally need something to cool them down. And what better than ice?

Drinks with plenty of ice simply taste better. The ice thickens the drink and gives it more 'body'.

Your ice should be prepared well in advance. It is important that it should look good, and is worthy of addition to your masterpiece. The cubes or blocks should be clean and fresh, and they should be as cold as possible. Remove cubes from the tray about an hour before you need them. Put them in a bucket or a bowl and replace into the freezer until needed.

If you want crushed ice, you can use a proprietary crusher or simply improvise. Many types of electric ice crushers are available in the shops, but you'll probably get more pleasure from doing it by hand. Put your cubes into a tea-towel or a plastic bag, and bash them with a hammer or rolling pin. If neither implement comes to hand, drop them on the floor and jump on them, or crack them into a nearby wall.

Always place your ice in the glass before the ingredients unless instructed otherwise. This cools your drink as soon as possible, and avoids embarrassing splashes which can occur when cubes are dropped into ready-prepared cocktails.

Exotic ice cubes can be prepared by freezing herbs and bits of fruit into the cubes. Simply fill your tray with water and sprinkle with the desired herbs or bits of fruit before freezing. To prevent all the 'bits' sinking to the bottom; half fill the tray, freeze the contents, pull the tray out and add your 'bits', top up with water, and then freeze the whole lot.

As a rough guide, when creating your own cocktails, use cubed ice for drinks which you don't want to be diluted. Use crushed ice for flavourful fruity concoctions, for straight liquor and for Juleps.

A small boy got up in the middle of the night to go to the toilet. As he passed his parents bedroom, he noticed the door was open and funny noises were coming from within. He took a quick peek and saw his mum performing oral sex on his dad. Interrupting proceedings he admonished his mother, "I take it this means you won't be taking me to the doctor on Monday because I've been sucking my thumb?"

THE COCKTAIL PARTY EFFECT

No, this isn't anything to do with losing your memory, throwing-up or getting laid. It is a real scientifically-acknowledged effect, that of selective listening. When you are surrounded by a variety of different conversations, like at a cocktail party, you are able to cut off your attention from all but one of the conversations.

Apparently your attention will be grabbed by someone uttering your name or a word that has special significance to you - such as "would you like a Slow Comfortable Screw?"

Scientists disagree as to how the brain is able to do this. Some believe all conversations are heard and processed by the brain, then one is selected for 'participation'. Others believe the conversation is chosen before the brain performs any processing.

Now, couldn't you bore the pants off a lot of people with that piece of info at the next party...

STEAMY GLASSES

... are the last thing you want. Your cocktail glasses should be clean and cool.

Make sure there are no greasy stains, no detergent residue and that they are completely free from odour. There is nothing worse than picking up a colourful, tempting cocktail and catching a whiff of warm plastic. Remember, even clean glasses can pick up smells from dishwashers and cupboards. Also, if you store your glasses upside down, the trapped air can become stale and ultimately affect your drink.

Keep your glasses in the fridge and take them out as you need them. This keeps the glass cool, and it doesn't warm up the drink when added. It also makes the glasses themselves look like an attractive addition to your lovingly prepared cocktail.

After the party, wash your glasses in very warm to hot water, rinse them under a warm tap. Put them all to one side as you wash the others, but don't allow them to drip-dry. Instead you should dry them with a cloth and use a different cloth to polish them.

Real glass always looks best when serving your cocktails, and it doesn't affect the taste of the drink like plastic glasses or tumblers. However, feel free to experiment with your serving vessels. After all, drinking cocktails is all about having fun!

Classic cocktail glass

This is the typical V-shaped, or triangular glass like the one on the cover. A long stem is best, since it helps you keep the drink cooler for longer. This is because you should hold it by the stem and not the bowl. If you hold the bowl, the warmth from your hand will conduct through to the drink. In addition, the glass will sweat and you'll get a wet hand.

This type of glass is best used for short and strong cocktails and holds around 90ml or 3 parts.

Old-fashioned

This is a standard flat-bottomed tumbler with sloping edges. It is normal used for straight shorts, shorts with ice. With cocktails, use it for similar short unstrained drinks. Holds around 4 parts.

Highball

This is a tall straight-sided glass. It should be used for long drinks with ice and those which are topped-up with lemonade or beer. Holds around 7 parts.

Champagne glass

These come as two different sorts. There is the wide rimmed bowl, not dissimilar to the classic cocktail glass with a deeper bowl. The bubbles from drinks held in these glasses disappear quickly, so the drinks should be 'downed' fairly rapidly. Quite a few creamy drinks are served in this style of glass.

Then there is the narrow rimmed flute, which helps keep the champagne bubbles in the drink by giving a smaller area for the bubbles to escape. The flute holds around 150ml or 5 parts.

Wine glasses

These come in all shapes and sizes. The standard white and red glasses are the most popular, with the only significant difference being in the size (the red wine glass has a slightly rounder bowl). They hold around 120-180ml, or 4 to 6 parts and can be used for a wide range of cocktails. Wide rimmed wine glasses go well with the more exotic drinks which require lots of garnish, umbrellas and twizzle sticks.

Brandy balloon

These have a short stem and a very large bowl. They allow the full aroma of the drink to escape, with the alcohol evaporating from the warmth of the hands. Very strong cocktails should be served in this style of glass, and those which look spectacular (perhaps containing cream or ice-cream).

Sherry glass

Short stemmed glass with a tapering, tulip shaped bowl. Holds around 2 -3 parts.

WORDS THAT RHYME WITH SCREW

ooh, who, blew, phew, ewe, view, woo, queue, spew, strew, slew, glue, clue, threw, flu, due.

INSTANT SEX

As early as the end of the last century a company called Heubleins were selling ready-mixed cocktails from their base in Harvard. Then as now, they were preferred by those who couldn't find the time to mix their own or who doubted their own proficiency at creating such delicious drinks.

Canned cocktails have recently experienced a resurgence in popularity, particularly in the USA. Around twenty different brews can be bought, and there has even been an attempt to launch 'powdered' cocktails in foil cartons.

AMAZING FACTS

The first true book of cocktails was by Jerry Thomas, who published The Bon Vivant's Guide or How to Mix Drinks in 1862. This was followed in 1882 by Harry Johnson's Bartender's Manual, or How To Mix Drinks of The Present Style.

The largest cocktail on record is a Pina Colada of 1486.6 litres, mixed in Germany in August 1988 by Kai Wulf, Ivano Birello and Axel Bornemann.

The most expensive cocktail you could make would be using a 60 year old bottle of whisky known as 'The Macallan'. This bottle was sold by the Rotary Club of Elgin, Grampian for £6,000 on 2 June 1988. It was bought by Sheraton Caltrust from Glasgow.

Alternatively, you could use the most expensive spirit available through retailers: Hennessy Private Reserve Grande Champagne which retails at £120 per bottle!

'The Cocktails' is Australian slang for having a dose of diarrhoea.

The first use of cocktails in a book and in its modern context appeared in Tom Brown's Schooldays with "Bill... the half-hour hasn't struck. Here, Bill, drink some cocktail."

To 'turn cocktail' in the military means to run away (cock the tail, turn and run).

A Cocktail in the 19th century was a slang term for a harlot. It could also mean a person who assumed the position of nobility but lacked thoroughbred status.

While Fizzes, Sours and Collins survive in today's recipes, the first books included sub-divisions of Twists, Shrubs, Daisies, Crustas, Smashes and Fixes.

A cocktail pianist plays light inconsequential music as a background.

Hop-scotch - the longest recorded hop-scotch marathon lasted 101 hours 15 minutes in Leicester during 1985.

If you find yourself short of ice, you could dig some up 250 miles from the coast of Wilkes Land in the Antartic. This is the thickest recording of ice on the planet at 2.97 miles or 4.78 kilometres thick. And if you are still short, why not chop a slither off the largest known iceberg sighted 150 miles west of Scott Island in the South Pacific ocean. At 208 miles long by 60 miles wide it had a larger area than that of Belgium.

Angostura is a flavouring agent used in some cocktails and super market fruit juices. It is derived from the bark of a South American tree, and has been used in several medicines.

The Cocktail Beetle, also known as the Devil's Coachman beetle, 'cocks up' its posterior when agitated.

Shochu are traditional Japanese spirits distilled from potatoes. They shot to fame in the cocktail world during the 1980s when they became the trendy drink for young up-and-coming Japanese. Cheaper than saké, Shochu were originally rough drinks for labourers and poor people.

The Hague Hash House Harriers - a group of perpetually partying runners - drink their cocktails out of a hollowed-out bulls testicle.

is shorthand for 'cocktail'.

O n their wedding night, Tracy went up to the bedroom to prepare herself. A few minutes later Sean arrived and knocked on the door. "Come on in Sean," giggled Tracy, "I'm not afraid." Sean paused for a couple of seconds and then replied, "You would be if you knew what I was knocking with!"

AMAZING CONCOCTIONS

● **Egg Ale** was a somewhat remarkable - and, on the face of it, a slightly revolting - concoction, although said to be highly nutritious, The old recipe stipulated:

To twelve gallons of ale was added the gravy of eight pounds of beef. Twelve eggs, the gravy beef, a pound of raisins, oranges and spice, were then placed in a linen bag and left in the barrel until the ale had ceased fermenting. Even then an addition was made in the shape of two quarts of Malaga sack. After three weeks in cask the ale was bottled, a little sugar being added. A monstrously potent liquor truly!

● **Eggnog** was made by gathering as many bottles of brandy as could be found in the house (and houses of relatives, neighbours and friends). These were poured non-too-gently into a large bucket which was placed under the nearest cow along with a three legged stool for milking.

The cow was milked into the bucket, and while the mixture was still warm, half a dozen eggs were cracked into the bucket. The stool was then up-ended and used to stir the cooling concoction into a traditional Eggnog.

- To make **Rumfustian**, a popular drink last century, mixing a quarter bottle of rum, the same of, a large bottle of beer, a bottle of sherry, 12 egg yolks, sugar, nutmeg, spices, and orange peel. Drink it and prepare for spontaneous combustion!

- **Flip**, a very popular drink for our ancestors, is made this way, according to an old recipe:

Place in a saucepan one quart of strong ale together with lumps of sugar which have been well rubbed over the rind of a lemon, and a small piece of cinnamon. Take the mixture off the fire when boiling and add one glass of cold ale. Have ready in a jug the yolks of six or eight eggs well beaten up with powdered sugar and grated nutmeg. Pour the hot ale from the saucepan on to the eggs, stirring them while so doing. Have another jug at hand and pour the mixture as swiftly as possible from one vessel to the other until a white froth appears, when the flip is ready. One or two wine glasses of gin or rum are often added.

- The **Domain Cocktail** was a lethal combination of pepper and petrol. It was popular with Australian vagabond drinkers from the Sydney domain in the 1940s.

- In 1949 an American newspaper reported that a girl had drunk two **Atomic Cocktails** in an effort to rid herself of a rare glandular ailment. Although the exact ingredients weren't listed, the brew certainly included radioactive phosphorus!

An old man wandered into a brothel. Switching on his hearing aid, he asked the madam for a girl. "How old are you granddad?" said the madam. "Eighty-five," replied the old man. "Eighty-five?" repeated the madam, "forget it, you've had it." The old man looked a bit bemused and then reached for his wallet saying, "Then how much do I owe you?"

SAYING After a few pints, every woman looks beautiful. After a few cocktails, all men are bastards!

BLUE MOVIES

Given the cocktail's close relationship with all things sexual, it is surprising there hasn't been a whole range of blue movies produced with the word 'cocktail' in the title. Instead, only two such movies are listed, and both were panned by the critics!

COCKTAIL was directed by Roger Donaldson in 1988 and the original screen version lasted 103 minutes. It starred Tom Cruise as a young runaway in New York with dreams of making a fortune from a chain of bars. He finds a job as a barman and is befriended by an old-hand at the cocktail game, played by Bryan Brown.

The introduction of a woman, played by Elizabeth Shue, into Tom's life causes the inevitable rift between the friends. Somehow the storyline contrives to arrive at a cocktail bar situated on an exotic beach where the two make up.

COCKTAIL MOLOTOV is French film directed by Diana Kurys from 1980. It attempts to portray the difficulty of being an adolescent while contending with the problems of becoming an adult. Elise Caron plays a young girl who runs away to Venice. Her boyfriend, Philippe Lebas, and his mate, Francois Cluzet, track her down and try to persuade her to return. She holds out until all her belongings are stolen and Lebas loses his car. The trio then return to Paris to join in the worker-student riots and to enlist in the ongoing political struggle.

The first cocktail served on stage was in the 1925 production of **SPRING CLEANING** by Frederick Lonsdale. This only just beat Noël Coward's **THE VORTEX** in which not one, but four cocktails made guest appearances.

LICK YOURS?

Liqueurs were originally made by monks in the 1300s and 1400s. Intended to be physician's healing remedies, these concoctions were first drunk for pleasure in Italy during the 1500s.

These days there are literally thousands of liqueurs around the world. Most are based on fruit, but others such as Benedictine, Galliano and Drambuie are herb based. The more exotic are based on plant leaves and nuts.

WHAT IS THAT YOU ARE PUTTING IN MY MOUTH?

Advocaat: A liqueur made with brandy, sugar and egg-yolks which give it a distinctive yellow colour. Originated in Holland and has a rich creamy body.

Amaretto: A liqueur made with almonds and apricots. Originated in Italy.

Anisette: A term used for any liqueur with an aniseed flavour. Usually very sweet and often colourless in its pure form. Popular in France.

Apricot brandy: Would you believe, a brandy flavoured liqueur made from apricots? Use it to soften bits of apricot fruit in your drinks.

Benedictine: A brandy based liqueur originally made by monks in Normandy. Amber in colour, it is very sweet and has a strong smell of herbs.

Blackberry brandy: A deeply coloured liqueur made from blackberries. Not to be confused with Cassis. Genuine Blackberry brandy is strongly alcoholic and is distilled from blackberries. However, brandy flavoured with blackberry juice is usually fairly soft.

Boilermaker: An American term for a shot of bourbon or scotch whisky followed by a lager chaser.

Bourbon: American whisky made from grain containing mostly corn. Gets its distinctive taste from the aging process made in charred oak barrels.

Campari: A bitter Italian aperitif.

Cassis: Made from blackcurrents softened in brandy. Crème de Cassis contains a lot of sugar and is best known for its use in kirs.

Chartreuse: Two very complex liqueurs containing around 135 different herbs. Green Chartreuse is the stronger in alcohol level and is also 'heavier' than yellow Chartreuse.

Cherry brandy: A sweet, sticky liqueur made from cherries and brandy.

Chianti: Dry red Italian wine.

Cognac: A high quality brandy from the Cognac region in France. The top quality is known as Cognac Champagne.

Cointreau: A colourless liqueur from France with a strong orange flavour.

Crème...   ***de Banane:*** A strongly flavoured liqueur made from bananas.
de Casis: From blackcurrants.
de Cacao: From cocoa beans, spices and vanilla.
de Fraises: From strawberries.
de Framboises: From raspberries.
de Menthe: White, green or red, peppermint flavoured.
de Mocha: From coffee beans.

Curacao: Orange, blue, white or green liqueurs made from wine, orange peel and sugar. Very sweet.

Drambuie: Scottish liqueur made from malt whisky and 'heather' honey. Irish mist is the equivalent made from Irish whiskey.

Dubonnet: A deep red French aperitif wine.

Framboise: Distilled Crème de Framboises.

Galliano: An Italian amber liqueur tasting of liquorice and lemon.

Ginger wine: Made from ginger and assorted fruits.

Glayva: Very similar to Drambuie.

Grand Marnier: Orange flavoured French brandy.

Grenadine: A sugary syrup used to sweeten cocktails. Non-alcoholic.

Kahlua: A Mexican liqueur made from coffee beans, cocoa, vanilla and brandy.

Kirsch: A sweet German brandy made from black cherries.

Maraschino: An Italian liqueur made by crushing the cherries together with their stones before distillation. Sweet and colourless.

Midori: A green melon liqueur from Japan.

Ouzo: Greek Anisette.

Pernod: Comes as Pernod 45 which tastes of aniseed and Pernod Pastis which tastes of liquorice.

Pimms No.1: Dark drink usually drunk with lemonade. Gin based. The most popular of the Pimms drinks.
> *No.2:* Whisky based.   *No.5:* Rye-whisky based.
> *No.3:* Brandy based.   *No.6:* Vodka based.
> *No.4:* Rum based.

Sabra: Unusual chocolate orange flavoured liqueur.

Sambuca: Italian liqueur made from liquorice and elderflower. Often drunk with toasted coffee beans.

Southern Comfort: peach flavoured American liqueur made with a brandy and whisky base.

Tia Maria: Mildly coffee flavoured Jamaican liqueur made from rum.

Triple Sec: French white Curacao.

Vermouth: simply a fortified red or white wine. Pure alcohol is used for the fortification and various herbs and spices are added for flavour. The alcohol level may be as high as that of sherry.

UN COCKTAIL

If you need something to tickle your fancy while you are in France, you may need the following phrases to help you get by...

Do you have any cocktails?
Est-ce que vous avez une queue de coq.

That was nice!
Cocorico!

Another Bloody Mary, please.
Encore une Mary de Sange, s'il vous plaît.

A slow screw against the wall.
Une visser lentement contre le mur.

A glass of Dirty Mother.
Un verre de Mère Sale.

That was strong!
Appelez un ambulance!

On the house.
Sûr la maison.

I need to cool down.
Est-ce qu'il y a une piscine?

I've spilt my drink.
Où sont les toilettes.

The drinks are on me.
Je voudrais transférer tout mon argent à vouz.

Of course I'm thirsty.
Est-ce le Pope catholic?

A Zombie please.
Cent francs de super, s'il vous plaît.

Three nuns were walking along the road. The first described with her hands the succulent grapefruits she had bought for the cocktail party. The second described the enormous bananas she had bought, also using her hands. The third nun, who was hard of hearing look at both of them and asked, "Brother who?"

THOMAS STEARNS ELIOT
(1888-1965)

Was a poet, critic and dramatist born at St Louis, Missouri, USA. He wrote many plays, including *The Cocktail Party* in 1950. Although Eliot is widely accepted to have exhibited intelligence and linguistic verve in his writings, *The Cocktail Party* was believed to have failed in its efforts to provide a unique setting for the display of Christian martyrdom. Thomas was born in the States, but he became a British subject in 1927 and died in London after gaining the Nobel Prize for Literature in 1948.

Eliot was born in St Louis, Missouri, and was educated at Harvard, the Sorbonne, and Oxford. He settled in London 1915 and became a British subject 1927. He was for a time a bank clerk, later lecturing and entering publishing at Faber & Faber. As editor of The Criterion 1922-39, he influenced the thought of his generation.

WORDS THAT RHYME WITH COCKTAIL

blackmail, exhale, toenail, telltale, detail, retail, hightail, bobtail, broadtail, ventail, bewail, avail, prevail, foxtail, resale, derail, hobnail, regale, impale.

A young army major went along to his first high-society ball. he was in deep conversation with a beautiful young debutante when her necklace fell off and dropped down the back of her dress. The deb fluttered her eyelids and asked the major if he could help her get it. Slightly timidly he complied and placed his hand down the back of her dress. "I can't find it," he whispered. "Try further down," replied the deb. But as he pushed his hand down, he noticed a lot of the other guests were starring at him. "Oh dear," he said, "I feel a perfect ass". "Never mind that," complained the deb, "just get the necklace will you!"

GIN

Basic gin is made by distilling pure grain with juniper berries. Various herbs and spices, including cardamon, coriander and angelica, are added at different stages of the process to give each make a unique flavour. Once bottled, the taste of gin changes very little.

More cocktails include gin than any other spirit. And by far and away the most popular cocktail of all, the Dry Martini, requires lots of it!

French 69

½ part gin, ½ part pure lemon juice, ½ part sugar syrup, Chilled champagne, Ice

Pour the gin, juice and syrup into a shaker. Shake well for 10 seconds and strain into serving glass. Top up with chilled champagne and garnish with a twist of lemon rind.

Blue Riband

1 part gin, 1 part white curacao, ½ part blue curacao, Ice

Pour all ingredients into a glass stacked with ice. Stir well and serve with a black grape.

Dunk It And See

2 parts gin, 1 part dry vermouth, ¾ parts Galliano, parts blue curacao, Ice

Pour all the ingredients into a mixing jug. Mix well and then strain into cocktail glass. Garnish with a red cherry.

Astoria

2 parts gin, 1 part dry vermouth, dash orange bitters

Gently shake ingredients with crushed ice. Strain into an iced cocktail glass.

Roll me Over

2 parts gin, ½ part lemon juice, ½ part Grenadine, ½ egg white, Ice

Pour all the ingredients into a shaker and shake for 10 seconds. Pour into a serving glass and garnish with a lemon wheel.

Gentle Lady

1 part gin, ½ part peach brandy, ½ part lemon juice, 1 egg white, Ice

Put all ingredients into a shaker and shake well for 15 seconds. Strain into a cocktail glass and garnish with a small slice of peach.

Queen Victoria

1 part gin, 1 part dry vermouth, 1 part apricot brandy, 1/6 part Grenadine, Ice

Pour the gin, vermouth and brandy into a mixing glass filled with ice. Stir well and then strain into the serving glass. Drop the Grenadine in and the red colour will spread through the drink. Garnish with a sprig of redcurrants.

Forever Green

1 part gin, ½ part dry vermouth, ½ part Midori melon liqueur, 1/6 part blue curacao, Ice

Pour the gin, vermouth and liqueur into a jug filled with ice. Stir well and strain into fluted serving glass. Drop the blue curacao into the centre and garnish with a sprig of mint.

Bartender

1 part gin, 1 part medium sherry, 1 part rosso vermouth, 1 part dry vermouth, ¼ part Grand Marnier, Ice

Pour all ingredients into a jug filled with ice. Stir well and then strain into the serving glass.

PM

1 part gin, 1 part Galliano, 1 part bianco vermouth, 1 part Campari, Ice

Pour all ingredients over ice in a jug. Mix well to cool and then strain into chilled serving glass. Garnish with red cherry.

Sing the Blues

1 ½ parts gin, 1 part blue curacao, juice of 1 lime, Ice

Put all ingredients into a shaker and shake vigorously. Decorate the glass rim by rubbing with a freshly cut lime. Pour drink into the glass and garnish with a lime wheel

Tango in Paris

1 part dry gin, 1 ½ part dry vermouth, 1 ½ part sweet vermouth, 2 dashes curacao, Juice of ¼ orange, Ice

Put all ingredients into a shaker and give a few short, sharp shakes. Strain and serve in a chilled glass.

Negroni

1 ½ parts sweet vermouth, 1 ½ parts Campari, 1 ½ parts gin, Twist of lemon peel, Soda water, Ice

Stir alcohol in a tall glass with plenty of ice. Top up with soda water and garnish with twist of lemon.

Frothy Delight

2 parts gin, 1 part maraschino, 1 part lemon juice, 1 dash Grenadine, 1 egg white, Ice

Put all the ingredients into a shaker and shake hard for 15 seconds. Pour into a large wine glass and garnish with a maraschino cherry.

Lady in Green

1 ½ parts gin, ½ part green Chartreuse, ½ part yellow Chartreuse, Juice of 1 lemon, Ice

Put all the ingredients into a shaker and then pour into a goblet. Garnish with a twirl of lime.

Golden Fizz

Juice of ½ lemon, Juice of ½ lime, 1 egg yolk, 2 parts gin, 1 tablespoon sugar, Soda water, Ice

Shake all ingredients except soda water in a shaker for 20 seconds with ice. Strain into a glass and top up with soda water.

Golden Dawn

2 parts dry gin, 1 part freshly squeezed orange juice, 1 part apricot brandy, Ice

Put all ingredients into a shaker and shake for 10 seconds. Pour into tall glass and garnish with a wheel of orange to greet the day.

Fog raiser

1 part gin, 1 part dry vermouth, 1 dash Grenadine, 1 dash Pernod, Crushed ice

Put the gin, vermouth and Grenadine into a glass with ice and stir vigorously. Drop Pernod into the top to swirl around on the surface.

British Bulldog

2 parts gin, juice of half lemon, 1 teaspoon caster sugar, Ginger ale, Ice

Fill up a highball glass with ice. Pour the gin, lemon juice and sugar over. Top up with ginger ale and garnish with the British flag.

Young Buck

Twirl of lime skin, 2 parts dry gin, Ginger ale, Ice

Put the lime skin (zest) in the bottom of the glass. Pour in the gin and then add the ice and ginger ale.

Caruso

1½ parts gin, 1 part dry vermouth, 1 part green creme de menthe

Shake ingredients with crushed ice or, alternatively, stir in a mixing glass with ice. Strain into cocktail glass.

Cherry Cobbler

1½ parts gin, 1½ parts cherry brandy, ½ part Creme de Cassis, ½ part lemon juice, 1 slice lemon, 1 teaspoon sugar, 2 maraschino cherries

Take a large glass and fill it with ice chips. Add the lemon juice and alcohol. Gently sprinkle in the sugar, stirring all the time to ensure it dissolves. Finally add the cherries and lemon slice.

Other Cobblers can be prepared using any fruit marinated in Amaretto.

Filby

1 part gin, ½ part Amaretto, ½ part Campari, ½ part dry vermouth, Ice

Pour all the ingredients into a mixing jug and give a thorough stir. Strain into a chilled serving glass. Serve with a sugar almond.

Black Italien

¾ part gin, ¾ vermouth rosso, ¾ Campari

Mix ingredients with crushed ice and shake. Strain into a wide rimmed glass and garnish with a cherry.

Foggy Day

1¼ parts gin, ½ part Pernod

Pour into a wide glass and add water to taste.

Gibson

2½ parts gin, ½ part dry vermouth, 2 cocktail onions

Stir gently in mixing glass with ice. Strain into cocktail glass. Add onions. Garnish with lemon peel.

Gin and Tonic

2 parts gin, Tonic water to taste, Lemon wedge

Pour into highball glass with ice. Stir well. Garnish with lemon wedge.

Gin Fizz

2½ parts gin, 1 part lemon juice, 1 teaspoon castor sugar, 4 parts club soda

Combine gin, sugar, lemon juice in shaker with ice cubes and shake. Strain into glass almost filled with ice cubes. Add club soda. Stir well.

Gin Seng

8 parts gin, 1 part lime or lemon juice, 1 part sugar syrup

Shake well with ice and strain into a glass.

Gin Sour

2 parts gin, ½ teaspoon castor sugar, 1 part lemon juice, 1 maraschino cherry, 1 slice orange

Combine gin, sugar, lemon juice in shaker with ice cubes. Shake well. Strain into glass. Garnish with cherry and orange slice.

Gimlet

1 part gin, 1 part lime cordial

Stir gin and lime cordial together. Serve in a cock-tail glass; if preferred partly filled with crushed ice.

Caribbean Sunrise

1 part gin, 1 part blue curacao, 1 part banana liqueur, ¼ part Grenadine, 1 part lemon juice, 1 part fresh cream

Pour the gin, banana liqueur and curacao into a shaker, and give it a short rattle. Open the shaker and add the lemon juice, cream and crushed ice. Give it all a long shake and strain into a tall cocktail glass. Add the Grenadine and garnish with a slice of pineapple.

Kiss in the Dark

¾ parts gin, ¾ parts cherry brandy, ¾ parts dry vermouth

Mix ingredients with crushed ice and shake. Strain into a wide rimmed glass and garnish with a cherry.

Marguerite

2 parts gin, 1 part dry vermouth, 1 dash orange bitters, 1 twist orange peel, 1 maraschino cherry

Stir well in mixing glass with ice. Strain into glass. Garnish with orange peel and cherry.

Great Barrier Reef

2 parts gin, 1 part Cointreau, ¼ part blue curacao, Raspberry ice cream, Angostura bitters to taste

Place all ingredients in a shaker, give them a good rumble and serve into a highball glass. Serve with a cherry.

South Pacific

1 part gin, ½ part Galliano, ½ part blue curacao, Lemonade

Pour gin and Galliano into a highball glass. Add ice cubes and top up with lemonade. Allow fizz to settle down and add the blue curacao slowly, allowing it to sink in the glass. Serve with a slice of lemon.

Martini

1 part gin, 1 part dry vermouth

Shake ingredients well with ice and strain into a cocktail glass. Decorate with a twist of lemon peel or a stuffed olive.

Martini Sweet

2 parts gin, 1 part sweet vermouth

Shake the ingredients well with ice and strain into a cocktail glass.

Martini Dry

4 parts Tanqueray gin, 1 part dry vermouth

Stir gin and vermouth with ice. Strain into chilled cocktail glass. Garnish with lemon twist.

Napoleon

2 parts gin, ½ teaspoon Curacao, ½ teaspoon Dubonnet

Stir ingredients with crushed ice and strain into a wine glass.

Pink Gin

2 parts gin, Dash Angostura bitters, 1 ice cube

Swirl bitters inside cocktail glass. Add gin, ice. Dilute with water, soda water or tonic.

Red Lion

1 part gin, 1 part Grand Marnier, Juice of ¼ lemon and ¼ orange

Shake all ingredients. Strain into cocktail glass.

Moon River

1 part gin, 1 part brandy, 1 part Galliano, ½ part Cointreau, ½ part lemon juice

Shake all ingredients together with ice. Serve in a highball glass with a slice of orange and a cherry.

Salty Dog

1½ parts gin, 5 parts grapefruit juice, ¼ teaspoon salt

Mix the gin and grapefruit, then add the salt. Stir and pour over ice cubes in a tall glass.

White Lady

2 parts gin, 2 parts cream, 1 part Creme de Cacao

Blend with crushed ice. Strain into a small martini glass.

Singapore Sling

Created at the famous Raffles Hotel in Singapore in 1915.

2 parts gin, 1 part cherry brandy, 1 part orange juice, Soda water, Dash bitters

Shake ingredients well with ice cubes. Pour into highball glass. Top up with soda. Decorate with pineapple wedge and maraschino cherry.

Blue Bijoux

1 part gin, ½ part dry vermouth, ½ part blue curacao, ½ part Galliano, Traditional lemonade.

Pour alcohol into a shaker. Shake with ice and pour into a highball glass. Garnish with lemon slice, then top up with lemonade. Some people like to add sliced mint.

Tom Collins

2 parts gin, Juice of ½ lemon, 1½ teaspoons caster sugar, soda water to taste

Shake the ingredients with ice and strain into a tall tumbler. Add ice, use soda water to top up. Decorate with cocktail cherries and lemon slices.

Union Jack

1½ parts sloe gin, 1½ parts gin, ½ teaspoon Grenadine

Shake all three ingredients with crushed ice and strain into a port glass. Traditionally drunk standing to attention.

Verboten Vrucht

1½ parts gin, 2 parts apple juice, 1 maraschino cherry

Shake the apple juice with the gin and a handful of ice cubes. Strain into a wine glass and add the cherry.

VODKA

Vodka is another spirit made from the distillation of pure grain. Like gin it is almost colourless, but unlike its great rival in the cocktail stakes, it is also flavourless. These qualities make it an ideal ingredient for most cocktails. Indeed, it can be used as a substitute for most of the other spirits without affecting the outcome too badly. What-is-more, drinking vodka very rarely produces that most feared of beasts - the cocktail party hangover.

The first recipes for making vodka were recorded in Russia during the 14th Century. Then it was made from the cheapest and most readily available ingredients which were suitable for fermentation. A couple of centuries later the potato became the preferred base, until this was later surpassed by cereal grain.

Most vodkas have an alcohol content of between 40% and 55%. Contrary to popular opinion, the Eastern Europeans prefer their vodka to be weaker than is normal in the west.

A Slow Screw

1 part vodka, 1 part sloe gin, orange juice

Place alcohol in a tall glass filled with ice. Top up with orange juice and stir.

For **A Slow Comfortable Screw** add 1 part of Southern Comfort. For **A Slow Screw Against the Wall** add 1 part Galliano, and for **A Slow Screw with a Kiss** add 1 part Amaretto. Obviously **A Slow Comfortable Screw Against the Wall** with a Kiss is one of the most powerful cocktails you'll ever come across!

Bloody Mary

1 part vodka, 2 parts tomato juice, 1/3 part lemon juice, Dash of Worcester sauce, Salt and pepper

Shake well with ice. Strain into wine glass. Garnish with celery leaves or a slice of pepper.

Godmother

1 ½ parts vodka, ¾ parts Amaretto

Serve in wide necked cocktail glass with plenty of crushed ice.

Lovers' Night Cap

1 ½ parts vodka, ½ part Drambuie, Dash Angostura bitters, Ice

Put all ingredients into shaker with crushed ice. Serve in traditional cocktail glass.

Hint of mint

2 parts vodka, 2 parts lemon juice, Sugar, Dash of creme de menthe, Mint leaves, Ice

Pour the vodka, lemon juice, and sugar over ice. Put a dash of creme de menthe into the glass and let a sprig of mint float on the top.

Lucky Jim

2 parts vodka, 1 dash dry vermouth, 2 dashes cucumber juice, Ice

Pour all ingredients all over ice. Serve in a traditional tumbler garnished with two wheels of cucumber.

Drunken Raspberry

1 pound (500g) raspberries, 1 quart (1.2 litres) vodka

Put the raspberries into the vodka and leave for about a week. Strain and put into a decanter. Serve the raspberries separately. They may look a bit odd but taste lovely. Strawberries or any soft fruit can be used.

Cote D'Azure

2 parts Vodka, 1 part lemon juice, 1 part creme de menthe, Champagne, Ice

Put all ingredients except champagne into shaker with ice. Strain into a tall glass and top up with champagne.

Silver Sunset

1 part vodka, ½ part apricot brandy, ½ part Campari, 3 parts fresh, orange juice, ½ egg white, Ice

Place all the above into a shaker and shake for 15 seconds. Garnish with a slice of orange, lemon and a cherry on a cocktail stick.

Red Rum

1 part vodka, 6 parts orange juice, 2 dashes Grand Marnier, 1 dash Grenadine, Ice

Put all alcoholic ingredients in a tumbler with ice and top up with orange juice. Serve with a maraschino cherry on a cocktail stick.

Kamikaze

1 part vodka, 1 part Cointreau, 1 part fresh lemon juice, 1/6 part lime cordial, Ice

Put all ingredients into shaker and shake for 10 seconds. Strain into a small fluted glass. Garnish with small gherkin.

Summer of '69

2 parts vodka, 1 part calvados, 1 part apple juice, 1 dash bitters, Slice of orange, Sprig of mint

Mix the vodka, calvados, apple juice and bitters in a tall glass with ice and give a good stir. Garnish with slice of orange and a sprig of mint.

Green Dream

1 part vodka, 1 part dry vermouth, 1 part melon liqueur, 1/3 part fresh lime juice, Ice

Crush ice and then place in shaker with all the other ingredients. Pour into a classic martini glass and garnish with a twist of lime.

Morning Dew

1 part vodka, 1 part Cointreau, 1 part blue Curacao, 1 part fresh, lemon juice, Ice

Put all ingredients into shaker and shake for 10 seconds. Pour into glass and top with crushed ice and a red cherry.

Weekend Relaxer

1 part vodka, ½ part Amaretto, ½ egg white, Grenadine, Ice, Fresh orange juice

Pour all ingredients except Grenadine into glass. Add Grenadine with a splosh just before serving. Garnish with Amaretto biscuit.

Bullseye

1 part vodka, 4 parts beef stock (cooled), 1/4 part lemon juice, Pinch salt and pepper, Dash worcestershire sauce, Ice

Place all of the above into a shaker. Shake vigorously for around 30 seconds and then pour into tall chilled tumbler through a strainer. Garnish with a slice of blood red orange and red cherry.

Black Russian

2 parts vodka, 1 part Tia Maria, Cola

Pour vodka and Tia Maria over ice cubes into whisky tumbler. Add cola to taste.

Black Eye

2 parts vodka,   part blackberry juice

Mix with ice. Strain into old-fashioned glass almost filled with ice. Stir well.

Blue Lagoon

1 part vodka, 1 part blue curacao, 4 parts lemonade

Fill a highball glass with ice. Pour vodka, curacao and then lemonade into glass. Stir and serve with cherry on a stick.

Hell Raiser

1 part vodka, 1 part Dubonnet, 1 part tonic water

Put ice into tall glass. Pour ingredients over and garnish with a small silverskin onion.

Screw-driver

4 parts orange juice, 1 part vodka

Pour vodka and orange juice over ice. Serve.

Chi Chi

3 parts vodka, 2 parts coconut cream, 8 parts pineapple juice, 2 scoops crushed ice

Blend all ingredients together with the ice. Garnish with a slice of fresh pineapple and a cherry.

Harvey Wall-banger

2 parts vodka,   part Galliano, 3 parts orange juice

Stir orange juice and vodka in highball glass with ice. Float Galliano on top.

Moscow Mule

1 part vodka, 3 parts ginger beer,   part lemon juice, 1 lime wedge

Stir vodka, ginger beer, lemon juice in highball glass with ice cubes. Garnish with lime wedge.

Vodka Fizz

2 parts vodka, juice ½ lemon, ½ teaspoon caster sugar, 1 egg white, Soda water

Put all the ingredients except soda water into a shaker and shake hard for 15 seconds. Put into tall highball glass and top up with soda water.

Russian Crush

3 parts vodka, Crushed ice

Simply fill a tall glass with crushed ice and fill with alcohol. You can make a Mexican Crush with tequila, French Crush with Pernod, and a Scottish Crush with whisky.

Fuzzy Screwdriver

2 parts vodka, 2 part schnapps, Fresh orange juice

Put alcohol in jug, top up with orange juice. Fill tall glass with ice cubes and pour screwdriver over. Garnish with sprig of mint.

Russian Cocktail

1 part vodka, ½ part gin, ½ part white creme de cacao

Stir vodka, gin, white creme de cacao with ice. Strain into cocktail glass.

Salty Borzoi

1½ parts vodka, 5 parts grapefruit juice, ¼ teaspoon salt

Mix the gin and grapefruit, then add the salt. Stir and pour over ice cubes in a tall glass.

Vodka Collins

2 parts vodka, Juice of 1 lime, 1 teaspoon caster sugar, Soda water

Shake well with ice. Strain into Collins glass with ice. Top up with soda water. Garnish with cherry and lime and lemon slices.

Vodka Dry

1 part vodka, 1 teaspoon dry sherry, 1 lemon twist

Swirl sherry in whisky tumbler to wet inside. Pour out remainder. Stir vodka into mixing glass

with ice. Strain into tumbler. Garnish with lemon twist.

Vodka Martini

1 part vodka, 1 part dry vermouth

Shake well with ice. Strain into cocktail glass. Garnish with lemon twist.

White Russian

2 parts vodka, 1 part Kahlua, Thickened cream

Pour over ice cubes into whisky tumbler. Pour cream over back of a spoon to form a thick layer on top.

Purple Love

1 part vodka, ½ part Parfait Amour, ½ part maraschino, Ice with lavender frozen in it

Pour ingredients into glass, adding vodka last. Use plain ice cubes. Garnish with sprig of lavender.

RUM

The Jamaicans will tell you that rum is a powerful medicine. They use it to treat cuts and bruises, to give relief from tooth and headaches, and even as a mild anaesthetic. However, anyone who has experienced Caribbean hospitality will tell you the sedative qualities can be far from mild.

Made from molasses or distilled from sugarcane, rum is delicious on its own, as a liqueur, or as part of mixed drink. The darker, sweeter rums from Jamaica are usually best drunk straight or in coffee. Whilst the lighter, dryer rums from Cuba and Puerto Rico work best in cocktails.

The first mention of rum as a drink appeared in records from Barbados in 1650. It was originally called kill-devil or rumbullion, but the shorter name of rum appears to have been in general use by 1667.

Daily rations of rum were given to British sailors from the early 18th century right up until 1970.

Wet Dream

1 part light rum, 1 ½ parts Dubonnet, ½ part lime or lemon juice, 1 dash bitters

Stir all the ingredients with plenty of crushed ice. Garnish with a raspberry.

Bossa Nova

1 part dark rum, 1 part Galliano, ½ part apricot brandy, 3 parts pineapple juice

Mix all the ingredients in a tall glass with plenty of ice. Garnish with a triangle of pineapple.

Carnival

1 ½ parts Trinidad or light rum, ½ part sugar syrup, ½ part orange juice, 1 teaspoon lime juice

Put all the ingredients into a blender with some crushed ice. Serve in a champagne cocktail glass with a garnish of a lime wheel.

Shanghai Dancer

1 ½ parts dark rum, ½ part anisette, ¾ part lemon juice, 2 dashes grenadine

Put the ingredients into a jug and stir with ice cubes. Strain into a cocktail glass and garnish with a wheel of lemon.

Apricot Lady

1 part Bacardi, 1 part apricot brandy, ½ part orange curacao, ½ part fresh lime juice, ½ egg white, Ice

Pour all the ingredients into a blender and blend until smooth and creamy. Pour into a tall wine glass and garnish with a slice of pineapple.

Bacardi Cocktail

Juice of one lime, ½ teaspoon sugar, 1 ½ parts light rum

Put all the ingredients in a shaker with cracked ice. Shake hard and strain into the glass. (Add a dash of grenadine if you want a pink version).

Hot Buttered Rum

1 small knob of butter, 1 teaspoon brown sugar, 1 part rum, Cinnamon Nutmeg, Vanilla essence, Boiling water

Mix the butter with sugar, shake of cinnamon and nutmeg and two drops of vanilla until well creamed. Place into a glass with a handle. Pour in the dark rum and add boiling water.

Between the Sheets

1 part rum, 1 part brandy, ½ part Triple Sec, Juice from ¼ lemon

Put plenty of ice into the shaker and add shake with vigour. Pour into chilled glass.

Phantom of the Opera

1 part white rum, 1 ½ parts grapefruit juice, 1 ½ parts curacao

Pour the ingredients over ice in a tall glass. Garnish with a paper umbrella.

Chocolate Cream

1 part white rum, 1 part dark rum, 1 part creme de menthe, 1 egg white, 1 part single cream, 1 tablespoon dark rum (for garnish), 1 teaspoon cocoa powder

Shake the white rum, dark rum, creme de menthe, egg white and cream with ice. Strain into a tall fluted glass. Float the dark rum on the top and sprinkle the cocoa powder over the top to decorate.

Sweet Daytime Sex

1 part dark rum, 1 part coconut cream, 1 part orange juice, ½ part fresh cream, ½ part sugar syrup, Strawberries

Pour all the ingredients into a blender, using as many strawberries as you prefer and adding the fresh cream last. Drop in a couple of ice cubes and blend until smooth. Strain into a large glass and serve with a chocolate flake.

Euphoria

2 part white rum, 1 part grapefruit juice, ½ part pineapple juice, ½ part curacao, Ice

Put all the ingredients into a highball glass with plenty of ice. Add a stirrer and garnish with a glace cherry.

Paradise

3 parts white rum, 2 parts apricot brandy, Ice

Place the ingredients into a cocktail glass and stir well. Garnish with a slice of fresh apricot.

Yellow Bird

1 ½ part Bacardi, 1 part Galliano, 1 part Cointreau, 1 part fresh lime juice, Ice

Place all the above into a shaker and shake for 15 seconds. Pour into a small chilled squat glass and garnish with a thick slice of lime floating in the drink.

Hot Egg Nogg

½ part dark rum, ½ part brandy, 1/4 part sugar syrup, 1 egg, Hot milk

Pour the rum, brandy, syrup and egg into a blender. Blend for 20-30 seconds and then pour into serving glass. Top up with the milk (heated in a separate saucepan). Mix well and decorate with a sprinkling of nutmeg.

El Dorado

1 part Bacardi, 1 part creme de cacao, 1 part coconut cream, 1 part advocaat, Ice, Desiccated coconut

Rub some orange juice (from slice of orange) around the rim of the glass and then dip this into desiccated coconut. Place other ingredients into a shaker and shake for 20 seconds. Strain into jug and then pour into serving glass taking care to preserve the rim arrangement. Garnish with slice of pineapple.

Fluffy Duck

1 part Bacardi, 1 part advocaat, Chilled lemonade, Cream, Ice, Sprig of redcurrants to garnish

Put Bacardi and advocaat into the chosen serving glass (try a wide shaped one). Fill with ice and then top up with lemonade. Mix with a stirrer and then pour on some cream. Pour over the back of a spoon so that it floats on top of the drink. Drape the redcurrants over the side of the glass for decoration.

Polynesian Pride

3 parts pineapple juice, 1 part Bacardi, ½ part blue curacao, ½ part lime cordial, ½ part Amaretto, Ice

Place all ingredients into a shaker and shake for 15 seconds. Pour into a Belgian beer style glass to give the illusion of a lagoon. Garnish with a slice of star fruit.

Daisy

2 parts Bacardi, ½ part fresh orange juice, ½ part fresh lemon juice, ½ part melted sugar, Ice

Place all the ingredients into a shaker and shake for 10 seconds. Strain into a wide rimmed glass frosted with sugar.

Boston Sidecar

1 part light rum, ½ part Cointreau, ½ part lemon juice

Shake well with ice. Strain into cocktail glass.

Cuba Libre

2 parts dark rum, Juice of ½ lime, Cola

Pour rum, lime juice into Collins glass. Add cola. Stir. Garnish with lime slices.

Coconut Blow

1 part dark rum, 1 part coconut cream, 1 part pineapple juice, ¼ part Amaretto, ¼ part maraschino

Put all the ingredients into a shaker with crushed ice. Shake vigorously and serve into a chilled champagne glass sprinkled with coconut.

Daiquiri

2 parts rum (light or dark), Juice of ¼ lemon, 1 teaspoon caster sugar

Shake well with ice. Strain into cocktail glass. Garnish with cocktail cherry.

Banana Daiquiri

1 part Bacardi, 1 part pure lemon juice, 1 part sugar syrup, 1/4 fresh banana, Ice

Put all these ingredients into a blender and blend until smooth. Pour into a cocktail serving glass. Garnish with a slice of banana (rubbed with lemon to prevent discolouration).

Gauguin

2 parts light rum, 1 part passion fruit juice, ½ part lemon juice, ¼ part lime juice

Place all ingredients into a blender and blend with a glass full of crushed ice. Serve in a wide rimmed champagne glass with slice of orange and cherry.

Grog

2 parts light rum, 3 parts water

Pour into old fashioned glass. Stir well.

Jamaican Shake

1¼ parts rum, ¼ parts Grenadine, 1 part pineapple juice, 1 part double cream, 1 scoop of chocolate ice cream, 1 glass of crushed ice, 1 wedge of lime

Mix rum, Grenadine and pineapple juice in a glass. Blend double cream, ice cream and crushed ice. Add alcohol and blend again. Serve in a tall glass and garnish with a wedge of lime.

Watch out Below

1¼ parts strong rum, 1 teaspoon Grenadine, ¼ part lime juice

Shake all ingredients with crushed ice and strain into a frosted glass.

Nevada

2 parts under-proof rum, 1 part lime juice, 2 parts grape juice, 1 part sugar syrup

Shake together all ingredients.

Pina Colada

2 parts dark rum, 2 tablespoons crushed pineapple, 3 tablespoons coconut milk

Blend with two cups of ice in electric blender till smooth. Stain into Collins glass. Serve with straw.

Planters Punch

1 part dark rum, 1 part light rum, 1 part anejo rum, 1 part lime juice, ½ part lemon juice, 3 parts club soda, 1 orange slice, 1 lime wedge, 1 pineapple wedge, 1 maraschino cherry, 2 teaspoons caster sugar

Shake rum, lime and lemon juice and sugar with ice. Strain into Collins glass part-filled with ice. Top up with soda water. Garnish with fruit.

Rum Cocktail

1 part light rum, 1 teaspoon Grenadine, 2 teaspoons fresh lime or lemon juice, ½ teaspoon sugar

Blend or shake together very well. Serve straight up in a cocktail glass or on the rocks.

Rum Collins

2 parts dark rum, 1 teaspoon caster sugar, Juice of 1 lime, Soda water

Shake well with ice. Strain into Collins glass ith ice. Top up with soda water. Garnish with cocktail cherry and lemon slice. Serve with straw.

Rum Crusta

1½ parts dark rum, ½ part Cointreau, ½ part lemon juice, 2 teaspoons maraschino liqueur, 1 tablespoon caster sugar, 1 lemon wedge, Spiral-cut peel of 1 orange, Crushed ice

Place sugar in saucer. Rub lemon wedge over rim of a wine goblet. Dip glass into sugar to thickly coat rim. Place orange peel spiral in wine goblet with one end draped over rim of the glass. Fill the glass with crushed ice. Shake maraschino liqueur, Cointreau and rum with ice. Strain into wine goblet.

Rum Fix

2½ parts rum, 1 teaspoon caster sugar, 1 teaspoon warm water, Juice of ½ lemon, Slice of lemon

Dissolve the sugar in the warm water and add the lemon juice. Pour this into a tall glass full of crushed ice at the same time as the rum. Stir and garnish with a slice of lemon.

Smiling Ivy

1 part under-proof rum, 1 part peach liqueur, 1 part pineapple juice, Dash lemon, Egg white

Shake together all ingredients.

Tiny Tim

1 part white rum, 1 part dry vermouth, 1 part pineapple juice, Dash of Grenadine

Stir with cracked ice

X-Certificate

½ part white rum, ½ part blue Curacao, ½ part lemon juice, ¼ egg white, 1 part champagne

Shake the rum, Curacao, lemon juice and egg white vigorously. Strain into a wide-rimmed champagne glass and top up with champagne.

Zombie

1 part light rum, 1 part dark rum, 1 part pineapple juice, 1 teaspoon caster sugar

Shake well with ice. Strain into Collins glass. Garnish with pineapple slices and cocktail cherry.

BRANDY

The best brandies, according to many, are those which are distilled from wine and come from France. The ageing process, carried out in small wooden barrels, gives it a distinctive golden appearance while adding to the flavour and nose.

A special type of brandy originates from the Cognac region of south-west France. The peculiar soil conditions allow a grape to be grown which only produces mediocre wine but which is perfect for the brandy making process. As with their famous sparkling-wine partners, Cognacs can appear as Grande Champagnes or Petite Champagnes. The term 'Fine Champagne' means a mix of Grande (at least 50%) and Petite Champagne.

Fruit brandies are made by crushing fruit, often complete with pips and stones included, into a mash and then fermenting the result. The best known of these are Maraschino made from cherries and the Spanish Calvados made from apples.

Brandy Alexander

1 part brandy, ½ part creme de cacao, 1 part thickened cream, Grated nutmeg

Shake with ice and strain into wide champagne glass. Sprinkle lightly with grated nutmeg.

Cafe Royale

Lump of sugar, Black coffee, 1 part cognac

Put a lump of sugar in a cup of good hot strong coffee. Add the brandy.

B&B

1 part brandy, 1 part Benedictine

Crush some ice, put in a warmed brandy goblet and pour the B&B in.

Brandy Fix

1 part brandy, ½ part cherry brandy, 1 teaspoon caster sugar, 1 teaspoon water, Juice of ½ lemon, 1 lemon slice

In a tumbler, dissolve the sugar in water. Add ingredients. Fill with crushed ice. Stir. Garnish with lemon slice. Serve with straw.

Brandy Flip

2 parts brandy, 1 dash bitters, ½ teaspoon curacao, ½ teaspoon sugar

Shake well. Strain into tumbler. Garnish with lemon peel and 1 sprig mint

Corpse Reviver

1 part brandy, ½ part sweet vermouth, ½ part Calvados

Shake well with ice. Strain into cocktail glass.

Southern Buster

1 part brandy, ½ part dry vermouth, ½ lime juice, Ginger beer

Put the brandy, vermouth and cordial into a glass. Add ice and stir, then top up with the ginger beer. Serve with a slice of lemon if desired.

Dirty Mother

3¼ parts brandy, ¾ parts Kahlua

Fill a short fat glass with crushed ice. Pour in the brandy followed by the Kahlua

Dirty White Mother

1 part brandy, 1 part Kahlua, 1 part double cream

Fill a tall glass with crushed ice. Add your cream first, then your brandy followed by the Kahlua.

Dirty Grandmother

3¼ parts vintage brandy, 1 part Kahlua

Fill a marbled or frosted effect glass with crushed ice. Then add your brandy and Kahlua.

Eggnog

3 parts brandy, 6 parts milk, 2 eggs

Take a large container and pour in your brandy. Add the milk and stir. Add eggs and blend. Pour into a large brandy glass. The same recipe can be followed with rum or whisky replacing the brandy.

Sidecar

1 part brandy, ½ part Cointreau, ½ part lemon juice

Shake well with ice. Strain into cocktail glass.

Stinger

¾ part brandy, ¼ part creme de menthe

Shake well with ice. Strain into cocktail glass.

Widow's Kiss

1 part brandy, ½ part Chartreuse (yellow), ½ part Benedictine, Dash of bitters, 1 cherry (black)

Shake with crushed ice and add a black cherry.

Brandy Smash

1 ½ parts brandy, 4 sprigs of mint, 1 teaspoon powdered sugar, Soda water

Crush the mint with the sugar in a tumbler. Add a splash of soda water, 2 cubes of ice and the brandy. Stir gently and garnish with a sprig of mint.

Yellow Fever

¾ part cognac, ¾ part Chartreuse (yellow)

Mix in a glass and add two ice cubes.

Pearl Oyster

1 part brandy, 1 egg yolk, Dash Worcestershire sauce, 2 drops tabasco, Salt and pepper to taste

Pour all ingredients into wide rimmed glass. Leave unstirred for mottled effect. Garnish with white onion (the pearl!)

Brandy Snap

1 part brandy, ½ part maraschino, 1 part fresh orange juice, Dash of bitters

Rub the rim of your serving glass with a slice of orange and then dip the glass into granulated sugar to coat it. Put all the ingredients into a shaker and strain carefully into the glass. Balance a cherry on a cocktail stick placed across the rim.

TEQUILA

Tequila usually comes as a clear un-aged spirit with around 40-50% alcohol content. The first tequila was produced soon after the Spanish introduced the methods of distillation to South America. It is made from pulque which is a fermented mash of the pineapple-like agave plant, and it gets its name from a town in the Julisco state of Mexico.

Mescal is a similar drink, also made from the agave plant, which is only distilled once, whereas tequila is distilled two times to maintain its purity. In some areas of Mexico, tequila is aged in oak vats to mellow the taste and to give it a pale straw colour.

Vesuvius

1 part tequila, 4 parts orange juice, ½ part Campari, Ice

Place ice in glass and then pour ingredients in the above order into a tall highball glass. Garnish with a black grape on a cocktail stick.

Mexican beach

1 part tequila, 1 part Tia Maria, 1 part dark rum, 1 part pineapple juice, 1 part coconut cream, Ice

Place all the ingredients into a shaker and shake well for 30 seconds. Put into a long lager glass and garnish with a sprig of mint with a cherry.

Highball

4 parts tequila, 1 part orange juice

Fill a tall glass with ice cubes. Add orange juice and tequila. Stir gently.

Other 'Highballs' can be made by substituting any strong liquor for tequila and any mixer for orange juice. To make a 'Lowball', simply use a smaller glass and halve quantities. A 'Softball' may be made by reversing the liquor and mixer quantities.

Margarita

1½ parts tequila, ½ part Triple Sec, Juice of half a lime

Shake the tequila, Triple Sec and lime juice with crushed ice. Rub the rind of the lemon on the rim of a stem glass, spin the rim in salt. Pour the drink into the glass and sip through the salt.

Mexicana

2 parts tequila, 1 part pineapple juice, ½ part lemon juice, 1 teaspoon Grenadine

Shake ingredients well with ice. Strain into a cocktail glass.

Mexican Bull

1 part tequila, 1 part Kahlua

Pour tequila and then Kahlua into an old-fashioned glass with ice cubes. Stir well.

Tequila Hooker

1 part tequila, 1 pinch salt, Wedge of lemon

Place the salt on the back of your hand and get your tequila at the ready. Now, quickly lick the salt, throw back the tequila and suck your lemon.

Corcovado

1 part tequila, 1 part Drambuie, 1 part blue Curacao, Lemonade, 1 lemon slice

Shake ingredients well with ice. Strain into a Collins glass filled with crushed ice. Top up with lemonade. Garnish with lemon slice. Serve with a straw.

Tequila Moonrise

3 parts tequila, 1 part dark rum, 1 part light rum, 2 parts beer, ½ part lemon juice, 1½ parts Rose's lime juice, 1 teaspoon caster sugar.

Shake all ingredients (except beer) well with ice. Strain into Collins glass with ice. Top up with beer.

Tequila Slammer

2 parts tequila, 4 parts lemonade

Pour the lemonade into a heavy-based (strong) beaker and carefully add the tequila. Now, cover the beaker with your hand, or a beer mat, and slam the drink on the top of a table. Drink in one go while fizzing.

Tequila Sunrise

1½ parts tequila, ½ parts Grenadine, 3 parts orange juice, 1 orange slice, 2 cocktail cherries

Shake tequila and orange juice with ice. Strain into Collins glass. Float about 4 ice cubes on top. Slowly add Grenadine, allow it to settle. Garnish with orange slice and cherries.

Viva Vegas

1 part tequila, ½ part lime juice, ½ teaspoon Grenadine, ¼ part maraschino, ½ egg white

Shake ingredients well with ice. Strain into wide champagne glass filled with crushed ice. Garnish with cocktail cherry, slices of lime and lemon.

The Riddle

1 part tequila, 1 part gin, Dash Galliano

Pour the tequila and gin over lots of ice stacked in a tall glass. Add Galliano to taste.

Boston Tea Party

1 part tequila, 1 part vodka, 1 part light rum, ½ part Cointreau, ½ part pure lemon juice, ½ part melted sugar, 1 part cola drink, Ice

Fill glass with ice cubes. Pour each ingredient, one at a time, into a tall highball glass. Stir well and when still swirling add double sprig of mint and serve.

Spanish Fan

1 part tequila, 1 part banana liqueur, 1/4 part blue curacao, Ice

Put tequila and liqueur into a mixing jug with lots of ice. Stir and strain into serving glass. Drop the blue curacao into the centre and watch it fan out. Garnish with a blood red orange wheel.

WHISKY
or BOURBON

Malt whisky is distilled from barley. This process is traditionally carried out over fires made from scottish peat and uses water from nearby burns. The minerals dissolved in the water and the aroma of the peat are said to give each malt its distinct flavour.

Since the late 19th century, a different breed of whiskies have sprung up. These are made by continuous distillation of grain. The result is then mixed with malt whisky to produce 'Blended Whisky'.

Both of these whiskies are matured in charred oak casks to produce the mellow flavours which scotch aficionados love. Blended whisky must be matured for at least three years before it can be legally sold, while malt whiskies are matured for around 10 to 12 years.

Obviously the longer process and greater attention paid to malt whiskies mean they are usually more expensive than blends. So, as with champagne, you should seriously consider using the cheaper alternative for your cocktails. Rumour has it, that in certain parts of Scotland, even putting lemonade in your malt is a capital offence.

Robby Burns

1 part Scotch, 1 part sweet vermouth, 3 dashes Benedictine, Lemon peel

Shake well with ice. Strain into cocktail glass. Garnish with lemon peel.

Hot Toddy

2 parts Scotch whisky, 1 teaspoon honey, Boiling water

Pour whisky into a strong glass. Add honey and then pour on boiling water. Pop in a slice of lemon and a cinnamon stick.

Blood & Sand

1 part Scotch whisky, 1 part red vermouth, 1 part cherry brandy, 1 part orange juice, Ice

Pour all the ingredients into the shaker and shake well for 10 seconds. Strain into a traditional cocktail glass. Garnish with a cherry.

Ladies Night out

2 parts whisky, 2 dashes Pernod, 2 dashes anisette, 1 dash bitters, 1 ice cube

Into a cocktail glass put all the ingredients and stir well. Garnish with a piece of pineapple.

Lady in Red

1 part Scotch whisky, 1 part red vermouth, Dash bitters, Ice

Pour all ingredients into a tumbler glass with plenty of ice.

Loch Ness

2 parts Scotch whisky, 2 dashes bitter, 1 teaspoon sugar

Shake ingredients with ice for 15 seconds. Serve in a cocktail glass garnished with a mini gherkin (the monster!).

New Yorker

2 parts bourbon, ½ part lime juice, ½ part Grenadine, Ice

Shake all the ingredients with ice for 10 seconds. Serve in a cocktail glass with a twist of orange.

Scotch mist

2 parts Scotch whisky, Ice, Lemon peel

Top a heavy based tumbler with shaved ice. Add whisky and drop in peel.

Dixie Stinger

3 parts bourbon, ½ teaspoon Southern Comfort, ½ part white creme de menthe

Shake well with ice. Strain into cocktail glass.

Pink elephant

2 parts bourbon, 1 part lemon juice, 2 dashes Grenadine, 1 egg white, Ice

Shake all ingredients well for 15 seconds. Serve into a cocktail glass and garnish with a fresh raspberry.

John Collins

2 parts bourbon, 1 part lemon juice, 3 parts club soda, 1 teaspoon, caster sugar, 1 orange slice, 1 maraschino cherry

Shake all ingredients except club soda with ice. Strain into Collins glass with ice. Top up with club soda. Stir. Garnish with cherry and slice of orange.

Manhattan

2 parts Canadian whisky, 1 part sweet vermouth, 1 dash Angostura bitters

Shake well with ice; strain into cocktail glass.

Kojak

3 parts bourbon, 2 parts passion fruit juice, 1 part pineapple juice, 1 dash dark rum

Pour all into a large glass with ice. Stir with a large 'lollipop'.

Manhattan Dry

1 part Canadian whisky, ½ part dry vermouth, ½ part sweet vermouth

Stir with ice, Strain into cocktail glass.

Fourth of July

1 part bourbon, 2 parts orange juice, ½ part lemon juice, ½ part apricot brandy, Ice

Shake ingredients in a shaker for 10 seconds and then pour into a heavy based tumbler. Garnish with a stars and stripes flag.

Mint Julep

3 parts bourbon, 1 teaspoon caster sugar, 6 fresh mint sprigs, stems cut short

Dissolve sugar with a few drops of water in highball glass. Fill glass to near top with crushed ice. Add bourbon. Garnish with mint on top. Serve with short straws.

Old-Fashioned

2 parts Canadian whisky, 2 dashes Angostura bitters, 1 lump of sugar, 1 orange slice, Twist of lemon peel

Soak sugar with bitters in whisky tumbler. Crush sugar with the back of a spoon. Add ice, orange slice, lemon twist. Add whisky. Stir well.

Irish Coffee

1 part Irish whiskey, 4 parts hot black coffee, 1 teaspoon brown sugar
Fresh cream

Put the sugar into the bottom of a glass and cover with Irish whiskey. Top with the coffee and mix well. Float cold cream on the top (by pouring it over the back of a teaspoon). Garnish with flakes of chocolate.

Whisky Sour

2 parts whisky, 1½ teaspoons sugar, Juice of ½ lemon, Soda water, 1 orange slice, Cocktail cherry

Shake well with ice. Strain into whisky tumbler. Add soda water to taste. Garnish with cocktail cherry and orange slice.

Rusty Nail

1 part Scotch, 1 part Drambuie

Pour Scotch onto ice in whisky tumbler. Pour Drambuie over back of a spoon so it floats on top of Scotch.

Flying Scotsman

2 parts Scotch whisky, 1 part sweet vermouth, 1 teaspoon sugar syrup, 1 teaspoon bitters, Ice

Shake all ingredients with ice for 15 seconds. Strain into a traditional heavy based tumbler.

World Cup tipler

1 part Scotch whisky, ½ part Cointreau, ½ part freshly squeezed grapefruit juice

Shake ingredients well for 15 seconds in a shaker. Strain into cocktail glass and garnish with red cherry.

Crazy Horses

1 part whisky, ½ part strawberry liqueur, ½ part banana liqueur, ½ part champagne

Shake whisky, liqueurs and ice for two minutes. Strain into a serving vessel and add champagne. Serve in a champagne flute with a small strawberry.

Boilermaker

2 parts whisky, beer chaser

Serve whisky in a tumbler with beer chaser on the side.

Irish Rose

2 parts Irish whiskey, ½ part Grenadine, Juice of ½ lemon or lime, Soda water

Place whiskey, Grenadine and juice in a tall glass with ice. Stir well and then top up with soda.

CHAMPAGNE

To call champagne simply a sparkling white wine from the Champagne region in France would rank as one of the understatements of all time. As a wine it stands head and shoulders above the rest, and as a way of celebrating there is nothing to compare.

For every connection made between cocktails and sex, there are two between champagne and good-living. Perhaps it was the traditional high cost of champagne that lead to its reputation as a drink for the well-off. But that certainly wouldn't hold any more. Many small houses produce inexpensive, excellent quality champagnes. Though a little younger than their dearer brethren, they certainly uphold the prestige of this Rolls Royce of drinks.

No other drink is paid the compliment of imitation as often as champagne. Other French regions produce 'mousseux' or 'methode champagnoise', the Germans make 'sekt, the Spanish provide 'cava', and the Italians offer 'spumante'. But non compare to the real thing. As a drink for special occasions it has no peer.

However, when it comes to cocktails you should consider these cheaper imitations. The whole point of drinking champagne is to savour the delicate, complex flavours produced by the expert blending of grape and cru. Mixing such a drink with curacao, stout or even orange juice would neither do justice to the champagne nor to your finances. Since it is the 'fizz' and the taste of wine you are after in a cocktail, why not use one of the many impersonations.

Buck's Fizz

1 part freshly squeezed orange juice, 1 dash Grenadine, 3-4 parts chilled champagne

Do not use anything but freshly squeezed orange juice for this drink as other wise your champagne will be spoiled. Put the orange juice into a tall champagne flute. Add the Grenadine and then carefully top up your glass with the champagne. Garnish with a wheel of orange.

Ritz Fizz

Chilled champagne, Dash Amaretto, Dash blue curacao, Dash pure lemon juice

Put all ingredients into a glass except the champagne and give a swirl. Then top up with chilled champagne and garnish with a twirl of lemon.

Arise My Love

1 Glass champagne, 1 teaspoon Creme de Menthe

Put the teaspoon of Creme de Menthe into a chilled wide rimmed glass (a flute will do but it's not so much fun!). Gently pour in the champagne.

Black Velvet

1 part stout beer, 1 part champagne

Pour simultaneously into champagne flute.

Sunrise

1 part fresh squeezed orange juice, ½ part orange curacao, Chilled champagne

Pour juice and curacao into fluted champagne glass. Top with champagne. Garnish glass with slice of orange.

Champagne Charlie

½ part Apricot brandy, Chilled champagne

Put apricot brandy into your chosen glass and top up with champagne. Garnish with a quarter of fresh apricot.

French Kiss

1 part Pernod, Chilled champagne

Pour Pernod into a tall long champagne flute. Top up with champagne and decorate with a twist of lime.

Naughty but Nice

½ part bourbon, ½ part fresh lemon juice, ½ part sugar syrup, Chilled champagne, Ice

Put all ingredients except champagne into a shaker. Shake for 15 seconds and then strain over the ice. Top with champagne and garnish with crysatalised lemon piece.

Bellini

2 parts fresh squeezed peach juice, 4 parts ice-cold champagne, 1 dash Grenadine

Put the ingredients into a large wine glass and serve immediately. Garnish with a slice of peach on a cocktail stick.

Black Velvet

½ glass chilled champagne, ½ glass chilled Guinness

Half fill a tall glass with the Guinness. Then slowly and carefully top the glass up with the champagne.

Blue Champagne

4 dashes blue curacao, 1 slice orange, 4 parts chilled champagne

Put the curacao into a fluted champagne glass and swirl to coat the glass. Pour in the champagne and decorate with the orange wheel.

Champagne Cocktail

1 lump sugar, 1 dash Angostura bitters, 2-3 parts champagne, Twist of lemon peel

Put the sugar lump into the glass and add the bitters. Add a twist of lemon peel and then fill the glass as required with champagne.

Norwegian Knockout

½ part brandy or cognac, 1 sugar cube, 6 drops bitters, Chilled champagne

Soak the sugar cube with the bitters and put it in the bottom of a tall champagne flute glass. Pour the brandy in and top up with chilled champagne.

Chicago

2 parts cognac, 1 dash curacao, 1 dash bitters, Champagne

Put all the ingredients except the champagne into a shaker. Shake and then strain into a glass. Top up with champagne.

Kir Royale

4 parts chilled champagne, 1 dash creme de cassis

Put cassis into the glass first and then fill with chilled champagne into a tall fluted glass. Garish with a sprig of redcurrants.

WINE

Spritzer

1 part dry white wine, 1 part soda water

Pour simultaneously into a wine glass and serve chilled. Sometimes garnished with twist of lemon and ice.

Sangria

1 full bottle dry red wine, 1 part Cointreau, 1 part Bacardi, 1 part brandy, ½ - 1 cup of sugar

Pour all ingredients into a large jug (sugar to taste) with plenty of ice. Stir well and add slices of oranges and lemons. Strawberries and raspberries may be added in season.

Quickie

1 ½ parts port wine, 1 ½ parts Grand Marnier, 2 dashes bitters

Shake all the ingredients together with crushed ice. Strain into a cocktail glass and garnish with a twirl of orange.

Kir

½ part creme de cassis, Chilled dry white wine

Pour the cassis into a chilled large goblet wine glass and add chilled dry white wine. Garnish with a sprig of blackcurrants.

Gluwein

1 bottle red wine, 3 tablespoons sugar, 2 slices lemon, 2 slices orange, 1 cinnamon stick

Place all the ingredients into a saucepan and warm through till on the point of boiling. Serve in a heated wine goblet and float a ring of orange on the top.

Crimean Cocktail

3 parts dry white wine, 1 part Cointreau, 1 teaspoon grated lemon zest, Soda water, Cherry, Ice

Place the wine, cointreau, lemon and an ice cube in a tall glass. Top up with chilled soda and garnish with cherries.

ODD-COCKS

With several thousand different liqueurs on the market around the world, there is an almost never-ending list of bases for your cocktails. In this category, you'll find those concoctions which do not fall into the sections owned by the cocktail heavyweights. Most will be outside the scope of the average amateur barkeeper, but they are still worth having a look at. If you see something that turns you on, it may well be worth a trip down to your local off-licence to place an order.

Wall Street

1 part Campari, 1 part Rosso Vermouth, Soda water, Ice

Pour Campari and Vermouth over ice into a small tumbler. Top with soda water and garnish with a cherry.

William Tell

1 ½ parts calvados, ½ part curacao, 2 dashes bitters

Shake the ingredients with crushed ice. Strain into a cocktail glass and serve with a slice of red apple.

Duke of York

2 parts Drambuie, 2 parts fresh orange juice, 1 egg white, Orange slice

Shake all the ingredients in a shaker and then pour into a cocktail glass. Decorate with slices of orange.

Braniff Special

1 apple, 1 orange, 1 peach, Juice of a lemon, 2 parts Kirsch, 1 strawberry

Slice the fruit into a glass bowl and cover with the lemon juice and kirsch. Allow the Kirsch to

marinate into the fruit (about 15 minutes). Serve in cocktail glass. Put slice of strawberry on a decorative skewer which can be used to spear the wonderfully flavoured fruit.

Golden Dream

1 part Cointreau, 1 part fresh cream, 1 part orange juice, 1 part Galliano, Orange wheel, Ice

Shake the first four ingredients in a shaker with ice for about 10 seconds. Pour into a tall glass and garnish with a slice of orange.

Hots for You

2 parts Cointreau, 8 parts hot tea, Orange wheel

Pour the liqueur into a tall glass. Add a long silver spoon. Pour in the hot tea and garnish with a slice of orange.

Nightcap

1 glass cold milk, 1 egg, 2 tablespoons honey, 2 parts cognac

Blend the milk, egg and honey by beating well. Pour into a warmed mug, add the cognac and relax.

Kirsch Kocktail

1 part Kirsch, 1 teaspoon castor sugar, 1 part black coffee, White of 1 egg

Shake all the ingredients in a shaker with crushed ice. Strain into a large cocktail glass and garnish with a maraschino cherry.

Mocha Flip

2 parts Tia Maria, 1 egg yolk, 1 tablespoon heavy cream, Shaved ice, Grated nutmeg

Place the Tia Maria, egg yolk, cream and ice into a blender or shaker. Serve in a wine glass and sprinkle with nutmeg.

Boys in Blue

1 teaspoon blue curacao, 1 teaspoon Pernod, 2 parts vodka, Sprig of mint

Mix all the ingredients with ice and pour into a cocktail glass. Garnish with a sprig of mint. (For variety you can replace the Pernod with Ouzo).

Pink Panther

2 parts Pernod, 1 dash grenadine, Soda water

Shake the Pernod and grenadine with ice. Pour into a tall glass and top up with soda water.

Kiss-me-Quick

2 dashes aromatic bitters, 1 ½ parts Pernod, 4 dashes curacao, Soda water, Ice

Put the bitters, Pernod and curacao into a highball glass with cracked ice. Top up with soda water and garnish with a red cherry.

Tiger

2 parts Pernod, 8 parts fresh orange juice

Mix together and serve in a highball glass with a ripe black grape.

Galliano Mist

1 part Galliano, Slice of lemon peel, Ice

Put all ingredients into a shaker and shake well for 5 seconds. Pour into a serving glass.

I Love You

1 part Amaretto, 1 part Kahlua, 1 part Bailey's Irish Cream, Ice

Pour the ingredients into a tumbler, one at a time over the ice. Stir in the glass and then garnish with a sprinkling of nutmeg and a Belgian chocolate served on the side.

Tornado Storm

¾ part banana liqueur, ¾ part peach liqueur, ½ part pure lemon juice, ¾ part dry vermouth, 1/4 part blue curacao, Ice

Put all ingredients except curacao into a shaker and shake well. Pour into serving glass and drop the curacao into the glass to create a storm effect.

Happy Times

½ part cognac, 1 part Cointreau, 1 part orange juice, ½ part banana liqueur, Ice

Pour all ingredients into a shaker and then strain. Garnish with a wheel of orange and a cherry.

Sweet Dreams

1 part Grand Marnier, 1 part cognac, Some orange wedges

Warm a brandy balloon glass. Pour the ingredients into the glass and then ignite. Let the flame burn for 10 seconds and then gently blow it out. Put your nose over the glass and absorb the wonderful smell.

Nova

1 part Galliano, 1 part rum, 1 part pineapple juice, ½ part brandy, ½ part lemon juice

Shake all ingredients together and serve in a highball glass. Garnish with pineapple slices and mint.

Gloom Chaser

1 part Grand Marnier, 1 part orange curacao, 1 part lemon juice, 1/4 part Grenadine, Ice

Put all the above into a shaker and shake for 10 seconds. Pour into a tall fluted glass and garnish with a half strawberry.

Melon Dream

1 part Galliano, 1 part orange juice, 1 part fresh cream, ¾ part cherry liqueur, Melon pieces

Place ingredients in a blender, and blend until mixture is rich and smooth. Serve in wide rimmed champagne glass.

Hot Love

1 part ouzo, 1 part green creme de menthe, 1 part red creme de menthe, 1 part fresh cream

Pour all ingredients into a shaker. Shake well and serve in a open champagne glass. Garnish with single black grape and mint.

Jelly Bean

1 part ouzo, ½ part blue curacao, ½ part Grenadine, Lemonade

Pour alcohol into a glass filled with ice and top up with lemonade. Drop a couple of red, green or yellow jelly sweets into the mixture as a garnish.

Silky Negligee

1 part Ouzo, 1 part Parfait Amour, 1 part green chartreuse, Ice

Place all ingredients in a shaker and shake well for 15 seconds. Strain into a serving glass. Garnish with a curl of orange.

Italien Stallion

¾ part Galliano, 1½ parts double cream

Gently blend with a glass full of crushed ice. Serve in white wine glasses.

Schnapps Zest

1 part schnapps, Bitter lemon

Pour schnapps into fluted glass. Top up with iced bitter lemon and garnish with twist of lime.

Schnapps Shiver

1 part schnapps, Tonic

Chill a stemmed wine glass. Pour in schnapps and chilled tonic. Pop in an ice cube with a twist of lemon frozen in it.

Peach Froth

1 part Grand Marnier, 1 part dark rum, 1 part pineapple juice, 1 part sweet syrup, 1 peach

Slice peach and place in blender with other ingredients. Blend until smooth and serve in a old fashioned glass. Garnish with slice of peach and cherry.

Peach Gold

1 part Grand Marnier, 1 part Galliano, 1 part pineapple juice, 1 part apricot liqueur, ½ egg white

Blend all ingredients into a smooth cream. Pour into a chilled highball glass and garnish with pineapple.

Red Eye

Equal parts chilled lager, And tomato juice

Pour together into a jugged glass. Allow a fair head of froth and garnish with a slice of red skinned apple.

Blue Movie

1 part Malibu, 1 part blue curacao, ½ part straw-berry liqueur, ½ banana

Blend ingredients with plenty of ice until smooth. Pour into a open champagne glass and garnish with banana slices. Suck through a straw.

Cream Sherry

2 parts cream sherry, 1 egg, Ice, Chocolate powder/nutmeg/cinnamon

Place sherry, egg and ice into blender and blend until smooth. Pour into a wine glass and sprinkle with chocolate powder, nutmeg or cinnamon.

The Butler Did It

1 part orange curacao, 1 part Southern Comfort, ½ part lemon juice, ½ part lime juice, Lemonade

Shake curacao and Southern Comfort with ice. Strain into a chilled highball glass. Add lemon and lime juice. Top up with lemonade. Garnish with mint leaves.

Lazy Screw

1 part vodka, 1 part Tia Maria, 1 part creme de menthe, Traditional lemonade, Fresh Cream

Pour alcohol into a highball glass half filled with ice. Stir. Top up with traditional lemonade. Pour cream over the back of a heated spoon so it floats on top. Garnish with a cherry. Drink through a straw.

B52

1 part Kahlua, 1 part whisky, 1 part Cointreau, 1 part fresh cream

Fill an old fashioned glass with ice. Pour Kahlua and Cointreau over the ice and stir. Top up with whisky and cream.

El Bango

½ part Kahlua, ½ part dark rum, 1 part coconut cream, 1 part fresh cream, ½ banana

Blend banana and alcohol in a blender. Pour into an old fashioned glass and add the cream. Stir and add ice. Garnish with mint leaves.

Tropical Affair

1 part melon liqueur, ½ part Cointreau, ½ part Blue Curacao, 4 parts orange and mango juice, 1 part coconut juice, Ice

Put each ingredient one after each other into your glass over the ice. Garnish with a chunky slice of pineapple.

Touch of Zam

1 part Sambuca (aniseed liqueur), 1 part Ben-edictine, 1 part Drambuie, 1 part orange juice, ½ part freshly squeezed lemon juice, Ice

Place all ingredients into a shaker and shake for 15 seconds. Strain into a champagne flute and decorate with a chocolate on a cocktail stick.

Comfortable Screw

1 part Southern Comfort, 1 part whisky, 2 parts milk, ½ part sugar syrup, 5 strawberries

Blend all ingredients until smooth and pour into a chilled glass with a couple of strawberries.

Japanese Slipper

1 part Midori melon liqueur, 1 part vodka, 1 part pure lemon juice, Ice

Pour all the ingredients into a shaker and shake for 10 seconds. Strain into a highball glass and garish with a slice of melon and a cherry on a cocktail stick.

End of the Piste

Tablespoon cocoa, Tablespoon sugar, 1 part Grand Marnier, Thick cream, Hot milk

Dissolve the sugar and cocoa in a small amount of hot water. Add the Grand Marnier and then top up with hot milk. Beat the cream until stiff and peaking and spoon on to the top of the hot milk. Sprinkle with orange zest.

Dizzy Blonde

2 parts advocaat, 1 part Pernod, Lemonade, Ice

Pour alcohol into glass over ice. Top with lemon-ade and garnish with a bright red cherry.

NON-ALCOHOLIC

For some reason, probably clouded in machismo, non-alcoholic cocktails, or 'softies', have a reputation for being insipid. But the truth is at odds with this assertion. A clever blending of strong and weak fruit juices, with other ingredients such as egg-white and chocolate curls, can make for a delightful experience.

When you are preparing for your party, remember not everybody likes getting legless. And for each group of friends who arrive by car, there should be at least one person who would appreciate something with a little more imagination than a can of lemonade.

Lady Penelope

2 parts orange juice, 1 part freshly squeezed lemon juice, 1 part freshly squeezed lime juice, 1 egg yolk, Dash Grenadine, Ice

Put all ingredients into a shaker, shake for 30 seconds and then pour into a flute champagne glass. Garnish with frosted raspberry.

Froth of the Wave

1 part freshly squeezed lime juice, 2 dashes Angostura Bitters, Lemonade, Ice

Frost the rim of the glass and then add all ingredients, topping up with lemonade. Garnish with a paper surfer.

Fruity Flip

4 parts freshly squeezed orange juice, 2 parts pineapple juice, 5 fresh strawberries, Small slice melon, Ice

Reserve half a strawberry for garnish. Place remaining ingredients into a blender and blend until smooth and ice crushed. Pour into highball glass, garnish with strawberry and straw.

Sunflower

2 parts orange juice, 2 parts pineapple juice, 2 parts lemon juice, Ice

Pour all the juices into a shaker and shake for 15 seconds. Put into tall lager glass and top with a black cherry (the eye of the flower).

Night of Passion

1 banana, 2 parts pineapple juice, 2 parts orange and mango juice, 3 teaspoons mashed passion fruit, Ice

Place all ingredients in a blender and blend until smooth. Pour into your chosen glass (try a wide necked champagne one). Garnish with pineapple slice (or freshly cut banana before it has coloured).

Aussie Cooler

2 parts pineapple juice, 2 parts orange juice, 1 part coconut cream, ½ part melted sugar, Ice

Pour ingredients in quick succession over a tower of ice. Use a long tall glass and garnish with a twist of lime.

Powder Puff

1 part fresh lemon juice, ½ egg white, Teaspoon Grenadine, Chilled lemonade, Ice

Pour the lemon juice, egg white and Grenadine into a shaker and shake for 30 seconds. Strain into a highball tumbler and top it up with lemonade. The resulting froth gives the drink its name. Garnish with dusting of icing sugar on the froth.

Santa Claus's Helper

1 part Grenadine, Lemonade, Fresh double cream, Ice

Pour ingredients in succession into the glass. Top to ¾ mark with lemonade and then slowly add cream over the back of a spoon. Cream should float on top. Garnish with chocolate holly leaf to float on top of the cream.

Cocktail Recipie Index

MORE HUMOUR TITLES...

The Ancient Art of Farting by Dr. C.Huff
Ever since time began, man (not woman) has farted. Does this ability lie behind many of the so far unexplained mysteries of history? You Bet - because Dr. C.Huff's research shows conclusively there's something rotten about history taught in schools. If you do most of your reading on the throne, then this book is your ideal companion. Sit back and fart yourself silly as you split your sides laughing! *£3.99*

A Wunch of Bankers
Do you HATE BANKS? Then you need this collection of stories aimed directly at the crotch of your bank manager. A Wunch of Bankers mixes cartoons and jokes about banks with real-life horror stories of the bare-faced money-grabbing tactics of banks. If you think you've been treated badly, read these stories!!!! *£3.99*

The Hangover Handbook & Boozer's Bible
(In the shape of a beercan)
Ever groaned, burped and cursed the morning after, as Vesuvius erupted in your stomach, a bass drummer thumped on your brain and a canary fouled its nest in your throat? Then you need these 100+ hangover remedies. There's an exclusive Hangover Ratings Chart, a Boozer's Calendar, a Hangover Clinic, and you can meet the Great Drunks of History, try the Boozer's Reading Chart, etc., etc. *£3.99*

The Beerlover's Bible & Homebar Handbook
(also in the shape of a beercan)
Do you love beer? Then this is the book you've been waiting for - a tantalising brew of fascinating facts to help you enjoy your favourite fluid all the more. Discover how to serve beer for maximum enjoyment... brew your own... entertain with beer... cook tasty recipes... and more! Includes an exhaustive listing of beers from all over the world with their flavours, colours and potency. You'll become a walking encyclopedia on beer! All for only £3.99

Down the Pan: Amuse Yourself in the Toilet
Do you have fun in the toilet? Or, do you merely go about your business and then depart? Instead of staring at the floor and contemplating the Universe, you could be having a ball! Here is an hilarious collection of *cartoons, jokes* and *silly stories*... a gruesome description of *great toilet accidents*... Discover the *secret card tricks*... Europeans may turn straight to the Franglais conversation sur la bog... Look at famous toilets of history... Learn to juggle toilet rolls! . £3.99

The Bog Book
(In the shape of a toilet seat)
How much time do you spend in the bog every day? Are you letting valuable time go to waste? Not any longer! Now you can spend every second to your advantage. The Bog Book is packed with enough of the funny, the weird and the wonderful to drive you potty. Fill your brain while you empty your bowels! £3.99

MORE GOOD BOOKS...

The National Lottery Book: Winning Strategies
An indispensable guide to the hottest lottery systems in the world. All designed to help you find those lucky lottery numbers that could make you rich. ı Learn how to *Play Like the Pros...* ı Discover ways of *Getting an Edge...* ı Improve your chances with the *'Wheeling Technique'...* ı Find possible ways of *Making it Happen* for you... ı See how understanding betting *Psychology and Equitability* can seriously *Improve Your Winnings...* ı Plus lots more *General Tips* to help you win! £4.99

Rude Cats (for cat lovers everywhere)
If you have ever wondered what your average moggie has been up to as it staggers back over the garden wall, covered in scar tissue and licking its rear end, then "RUDE CATS" is for you. Join Randy, an old campaigner on a sexually explicit journey of discovery into the twilight world beyond the cat-flap and prepare to be shocked! £3.99

The Armchair Guide to Football
An inexpensive and humorous look at the state of modern football. Is it really run by money crazed businessmen who don't care about tradition? Will Fantasy Football remove the need for pitches, players and footballs? Only £1.99

The Armchair Guide to Fishing
Just why do people go fishing? Is it the basic hunting instinct or do they just love drowning maggots? Only £1.99

The Armchair Guide to Golf
From the serious handicap hunter to the weekend hacker, everybody involved with golf will appreciate this humorous view from the 'inside'. Only £1.99

For a free full colour catalogue of all titles, please send an SAE to the address below.